BOSTON

Foot Notes
A Walking Guide

BOSTON

Foot Notes
A Walking Guide

REVISED 2ND EDITION

Jane Grossman and Felice Yager

Illustrations by Robert Bowden

The Countryman Press
Woodstock, Vermont

THE BACK BAY POLKA (from "The Shocking Miss Pilgrim")
Music and Lyrics by GEORGE GERSHWIN and IRA GERSHWIN
© 1946 (Renewed) GEORGE GERSHWIN MUSIC
and IRA GERSHWIN MUSIC
All Rights Administered by WB MUSIC CORP.
All Rights Reserved
Used by Permission of ALFRED PUBLISHING CO., INC.

Illustrations by Robert Bowden
Maps by Vern Associates

Edited, composed, and designed by Vern Associates, Inc., www.vernassoc.com

ISBN 978-0-88150-888-8

Published by The Countryman Press
P.O. Box 748, Woodstock, VT 05091
Distributed by W. W. Norton & Company, Inc.
500 Fifth Avenue, New York, NY 10110

Printed in the United States of America

Second edition
10 9 8 7 6 5 4 3 2 1

Dedication

For Molly
Our faithful four-footed friend, whose daily
morning walk inspired this book

Contents

Acknowledgments

Special thanks to: Audrey Cohen for introducing us; Kitty Benedict, Ellen Citron, Susan Knight, Dale Mnookin, Rona Roberts, and Susan Sidel for test-walking; Edgar Driscoll, Susan Dunbar, Jody Eldridge, David Garber, Maria Karagianis, Toni Norton, Louise Packard, Gail Roberts, Steve Ross, Tom Trowbridge, and Ken Tutunjian for their observations and insights; Peter Blaiwas, Brian Hotchkiss, and Ben Jenness for their excellent editorial and design sensibilities; our mothers, Belle Bernstein and Flossy Silverman, who believed in the project and "walked" vicariously; our children, Alaine, Alison, Andrew, Jess, John, Kate, and Matthew for inspiration; and most especially our husbands, Allen Grossman and Henry Yager, for their enthusiasm, encouragement, and love.

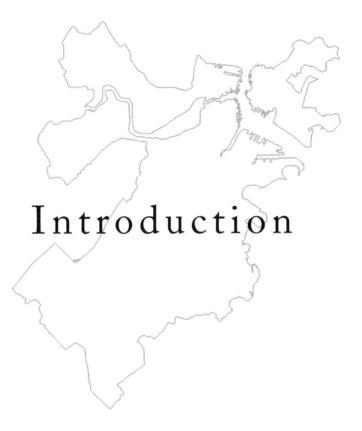

Introduction

The author Oliver Wendell Holmes may have exaggerated when he dubbed Boston "the hub of the solar system," but it is no overstatement to say that Boston is the best walking city in America. For the past 375 years, Bostonians have walked. In the beginning, it was because few other options existed. Now it is because walking is so pleasurable. And one *has* to walk—the driving is impossible ...

Like many great cities, Boston has multiple personalities, represented by various neighborhoods. We have chosen to guide you through those we have found to be the most colorful and unique—our favorites. As different as the routes may seem, they have a unifying theme—the evolution of Boston's character: a combination of history, society, and architecture. Though the text does "walk" you through the defining features of different architectural styles, an emphasis on people animates the book. For example, it points out not just where George Washington slept, but why he was there.

For locals, this book will introduce you to former residents who may be unfamiliar and streets and sites you may never have noticed. For visitors, this book will give you a real sense of life in Boston today as well as three centuries ago.

The walks range from 2 1/4 to 3 1/2 hours in length. Before setting off on a walk, read the essential information at the beginning of the chapter and check for addenda at the end of the chapter. You can easily spend a whole day in each neighborhood, utilizing the supplementary recommendations. Conversely, following the routes we have suggested, two walks can be comfortably combined. Although we do not recommend specific restaurants and shops (they change too often), we do direct you to streets where we eat and shop. There are public buildings and commercial establishments on each walk; a polite request will help you gain access to bathrooms. All information regarding days and hours of operation for the places of interest cited in the text are up-to-date as of this printing; however, we do suggest confirming this information using the phone numbers provided. Numbers in **boldface type** in square brackets correspond to the numbers on the maps. Sidebar directions will also help to keep you on track. Finally, in the event of rain, consulting Indoor Foot Notes at the back of the book will yield numerous bad-weather options.

The walks are presented alphabetically—there is no "right" order in which to tour. The following is a quick synopsis of each walk so you can choose according to your mood, energy, and time constraints.

BACK BAY: The ultimate landfill. This area, reclaimed from the sea, was successfully planned as Boston's most elegant and cultured neighborhood. A virtual museum of Victorian architecture, it includes Trinity Church, consistently counted among America's top ten most beautiful buildings. (2 ¼ hours)

BEACON HILL: This is quintessential red-brick Boston, with its charming Federal architecture, its narrow streets, and its gossip, both real and implausible. Here, money was made, styles were set, and ideals were promulgated, all in typical understated Boston style. (2 ¼ hours)

CAMBRIDGE: This academic powerhouse across the Charles River has been shaping minds since 1636 and influencing Bostonians for almost as long. But there is more to Cambridge than Harvard—we are biased, for we both live here—a colonial history, appealing architecture, and the river. (2 ½ hours)

DOWNTOWN AND NORTH END: Downtown buzzes with contrasts: momentous historical events, avant-garde architecture, and the convivial Quincy Market. The self-contained Italian North End, with its village character, is a wonderful counterpoint. This walk can easily be divided in two. (3 ½ hours)

WATERFRONT AND CHARLESTOWN: And this is where Boston got its start. Highlighted by a crucial Revolutionary War battle site, warships, taverns, and the clipper trade, this "walk" includes a 10-minute boat ride from Boston Harbor to the Charlestown Navy Yard and an introduction to the new Rose Kennedy Greenway. (2 ½ hours)

We hope you enjoy Boston as much as we do. We planned the routes so that both newcomers and residents would enjoy the sights, savor the history, and appreciate the people who have made Boston the city we love.

Some last cautionary words before you set off: Always cross at traffic lights or crosswalks. Boston drivers are notorious for their lax attention to rules of the road, so be especially careful. Don't hesitate to wear comfortable shoes and clothing; Boston is a casual city with numerous brick and cobblestone walkways.

CAMBRIDGE

WATERFRONT
CHARLESTOWN

3

5

2

4

1

BACK BAY

BEACON HILL

DOWNTOWN
NORTH END

BOSTON
AND
CAMBRIDGE

N

Back Bay

"I've got the best architect in Boston . . .
and if money can do it, I guess
I'm going to be suited."
—William Dean Howells, *The Rise of Silas Lapham*

Essential Information for Walk One

Length of walk:	2 miles
Terrain:	flat
Time:	2 ¼ hours at a leisurely pace, without going inside any of the buildings
Nearest T stop:	Arlington Street on Green Line
Starting point:	Exit T and cross Arlington Street; walk left to main Public Garden gate across from Commonwealth Avenue Mall

Supplements to the Walk

Highly Recommended

Guided tour of Gibson House
Time:	45 minutes
Hours:	Wed.–Sun., 1:00, 2:00, and 3:00 P.M. except holidays
Telephone:	617-267-6338
Admission:	$7; discount for seniors, students, and children
When:	first third of walk at #137 Beacon Street

Visit to Boston Public Library
Time:	15–30 minutes
Hours:	Mon.–Thurs., 9:00 A.M.– 9:00 P.M.; Fri.–Sat., 9:00 A.M.– 5:00 P.M., Sun., 1:00–5:00 P.M., Oct.–May only
Telephone:	617-536-5400
Admission:	free
When:	last third of walk at Copley Square

Self-guided or docent-led tour of Trinity Church
Time:	25–50 minutes
Hours:	Self-guided: Tues.–Sat., 9:00 A.M.– 6:00 P.M.; docent-led tours call for schedule
Telephone:	617-536-0944
Admission:	$6; discount for seniors and students
When:	end of walk at Copley Square

Browse and lunch on Newbury Street

Of Further Interest

Trinity Church Rectory at #233 Clarendon Street
Designed by H. H. Richardson, his style and originality are easily recognizable. This building still
houses the rector of Trinity.

Time:	5 minutes
Hours:	all day
When:	on the way to Newbury Street

Stroll through Boston Public Garden

Time:	25–35 minutes
Hours:	all day
When:	at end of walk

Stroll along Charles River Esplanade

Time:	25–35 minutes
Hours:	all day
When:	at end of walk; take Clarendon Street to Storrow Drive and cross footbridge between Clarendon Street and Dartmouth Street

Back Bay - Walk One

1. Public Garden
2. Lagoon
3. Footbridge
4. Statue of George Washington
5. #1, #3, and #5 Comm. Ave.
6. #20 Comm. Ave.
7. #25–#27 Comm. Ave.
8. #29 Comm. Ave.—Haddon Hall
9. First and Second Church
10. #137 Beacon Street—Gibson House
11. #150–#152 Beacon Street
12. #180 Beacon Street
13. First Baptist (Brattle Square) Church
14. #121 Comm. Ave.
15. #128 and #130 Comm. Ave.
16. #152 Comm. Ave.—Chilton Club
17. Hotel Vendome Fire Memorial
18. Hotel Vendome
19. #306 Dartmouth Street—Ames-Webster House
20. #315 Dartmouth Street—Hollis H. Hunnewell House
21. #163–#165 Marlborough Street—Cushing-Endicott House; #164—Crowninshield House
22. #191 and #196 Marlborough Street
23. Fairfield Street
24. #217 Comm. Ave.—Algonquin Club; #199—St. Botolph Club
25. #191 Comm. Ave.—Hotel Agassiz
26. #270 Dartmouth Street—Boston Art Club
27. New Old South Church
28. Boston Public Library
29. Copley Plaza Hotel
30. John Hancock Tower
31. Trinity Church
32. Statue of Tortoise and Hare

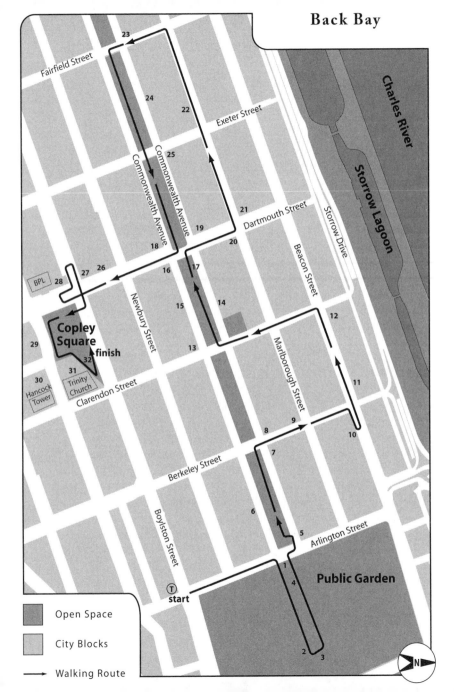

Back Bay

Charles River

Storrow Lagoon

Fairfield Street

Exeter Street

Dartmouth Street

Storrow Drive

Beacon Street

Commonwealth Avenue

Commonwealth Avenue

BPL

Copley Square

finish

Newbury Street

Marlborough Street

Hancock Tower

Trinity Church

Clarendon Street

Berkeley Street

Boylston Street

Arlington Street

Public Garden

(T) **start**

Open Space

City Blocks

→ Walking Route

N

The up and coming who shared space with the ancestrally endowed.

—Jane Holtz Kay, *Lost Boston*

Cleveland Amory, chronicler of 20th-century American mores, relates the following apocryphal but very conceivable story in *The Proper Bostonians.*

In the palmy days of the twenties [1920s] a Chicago banking house asked the Boston invest-ment firm of Lee, Higginson and Co. for a letter of recommendation about a young Bostonian they were considering employing. Lee, Higginson could not say enough for the young man. His father, they wrote, was a Cabot, his mother a Lowell; further back his background was a happy blend of Salton-stalls, Appletons, Peabodys and other of Boston's First Families. The recommendation was given without hesitation. Several days later came a curt acknowledgement from Chicago. Lee, Higginson was thanked for its trouble. Unfortunately, how-ever, the material supplied on the young man was not exactly of the type the Chicago firm was seek-ing. "We were not," their letter declared, "contem-plating using Mr. _____ for breeding purposes."

👣

Enter Public Garden; walk to edge of lagoon

The Back Bay is where the great old families of Boston collided and coexisted with the burgeon-ing middle class of the industrial revolution. The Public Garden and the adjacent Common (see Beacon Hill Walk) visually and philosophically represent this very Bostonian schism. Formal and structured, the **Public Garden [1]** is made for promenades. Relaxed and natural, the Common is made for touch football and Frisbee.

But in 1824, only the Common existed as civic space. The 24 acres that now comprise the Public Garden lay at the far-western edge of town—a dreadful place where no proper Bostonian would set foot. This was a marshy flat, home to dangerous rope factories that often caught fire. When the last factory burned down, opportunistic businessmen lobbied to build housing, but they were overruled by the town fathers, who decreed that the area be kept "open for the circulation of air from the West for the sake of the health of the citizens." A group of wealthy horticultural enthusiasts pursued the idea of a European garden, built a grand conservatory nearby, and in 1837 envisioned the first botanical garden in America; yet it took over 20 years for the idea to take root. Landscape architect George Meacham designed today's winding paths, flowerbeds, and little lagoon. If the Common is reminiscent of rural England, then the Public Garden's lineage is royal French. Although inspired by Versailles, these manicured flowerbeds and perfectly placed trees were created for public appreciation . . . but no walking on the grass!

This whimsical **lagoon [2]** is familiar to duck lovers around the world as the destination of the Mallard family: here the famous offspring in Robert McCloskey's childhood favorite, *Make Way for Ducklings,* were reunited with their father. Equally endearing to the children of Boston are the famous swan boats, whose family has grown from the original 1877 catamaran to the current "flock" of six. Hatched by English-man Robert Paget, a laborer at the Charlestown Navy Yard, they were inspired by his love of the Wagnerian opera *Lohengrin,* in which the hero comes to the rescue of his damsel in a swan-drawn boat. The first craft was built of wood, copper, and bicycle parts; today they are made of fiberglass, but like the prototype they are still pedal-powered. These "swansations" grace the pond from mid-April to mid-September. For over one hundred years, they have been nurtured and tended by the Paget family.

The little **footbridge [3],** a delightful visual con-coction, was actually built to resolve a commuting problem. As real estate development flourished in Back Bay, new residents needed a shortcut across the lagoon to walk to their downtown offices. Completed in 1867, it was a miniature epitome of modernity, a suspension bridge. (Technically, it is no longer a suspension bridge because of struc-tural repairs.) Nicknamed the "Bridge of Size," due to its pretensions of grandeur, it still evokes sighs of pleasure in the hearts of Bostonians.

Return to eques-trian statue at entrance

These Victorian meandering pathways explode in riots of color, and yet the spectacular flowers are contained in very well-behaved beds. The Public Garden was the first American home of the tulip; though no longer considered exotic, at that time it was a rare import. Today, the rotating seasonal plantings are labeled with botanical species and family names, from the patrician tropicals to the plebeian pansies—for, according to *Boston Ways* author, George F. Weston Jr., "In Boston, family is important, even in the vegetable kingdom."

The father of our country is commemorated by a grand **equestrian statue [4],** a 38-foot monument that powerfully captures the elegant horsemanship of our first president. His composure and confidence are apparent in his facial expression, his posture, and his unruffled control over the muscled stallion he rides. Although Washington is usually portrayed upon a white horse, this mighty steed was carefully modeled after a Boston warhorse named Black Prince. The statue was created by local sculptor Thomas Ball, cast by a nearby foundry, and sits on a Massachusetts-granite base—it is indeed homegrown.

Exit Garden gate: stand on Arlington Street facing straight ahead, up Commonwealth Avenue

Yet Washington never actually rode where he now stands. This cityscape was once under water, a place for fishing, bathing, and skating. In fact, it was from here that the redcoats sailed across the Charles River to launch their attack on Lexington and Concord. This was "the sea" as in "One if by land and two if by sea." In fact, all of this area is reclaimed from the sea; its name literally represents what it was—Boston's back bay before it became Boston's Back Bay. As you look at the urban panorama before you, it is hard to believe that just over 150 years ago water extended from the tall buildings rising on your left all the way to the Charles River three blocks to your right.

Unfortunately, whenever the tide receded, the swampy back bay became malodorous indeed, with "every Western wind sending its pestilential exhalations across the entire city." After the area was declared a health hazard in 1849, plans for its rehab began to take shape—filling in 450 acres of offensive marsh. Ironically, just 25 years earlier, the space for the Public Garden had been set aside to provide citizens with access to the salubrious western air.

An enormous and ambitious project, Boston's first Big Dig (see Downtown and North End Walk) could not have happened without the invention of the steam shovel. Two of these amazing new machines worked nonstop for 30 years, digging dirt and gravel in nearby Needham. In 1858, *The Saturday Evening Gazette* described the scene:

> *145 dirt cars, with 80 men, including engineers, brakemen and all, are employed night and day in loading and transporting the gravel over the road. The trains consist of 35 cars each and make, in the day time, 16 trips, and in the night 9 or 10, or 25 in 24 hours. Three trains are continually on the road during the day, and one arrives at the Back Bay every 45 minutes. At this rate, the operation moved about 2500 cubic yards a day, enough to fill 2 house lots.*

Each house lot was auctioned off the very day it was completed.

Because the Back Bay was conceptualized before a single dwelling had been built, the area exemplifies urban planning at its best. The neighborhood was to project genteel order and grace: harmony would be achieved by mandating consistent height, setback, and building materials; the streets were to be wide, with land set aside for cultural and religious institutions. Houses were not placed randomly but rather in an ordered sequence, east to west, beginning here at Arlington

Street. Following this route, you can observe the development of 19th-century architectural styles. The first blocks reflect a Francophile influence, the next a more fanciful Victorian, and the final phase ultimately turns to a classical bias. This pattern is interrupted by very few exceptions. The area is a virtual museum; in fact, it is the largest aggregate of such houses still in use in America today.

These homes were occupied by both Brahmins (Boston's elite and socially prominent First Families, so named by Oliver Wendell Holmes) and the new wealthy merchant class. Yet geography managed to maintain Boston's traditional social strata. The most desirable address was Beacon Street, known as home to those who had both pedigree and purse; next was Marlborough Street, for those with pedigree but not purse; Commonwealth Avenue was home to those with purse but not pedigree; and Newbury Street was the address for those who had neither. And within these categories, the most coveted homes stood on the river side of Beacon Street and the sunny side of Commonwealth Avenue.

The elegance of **Comm. Ave.** (Bostonians rarely use its full name) reflects the vision and personality of its cosmopolitan architect, Arthur Gilman. High-society Boston was enamored of all things French, from building design to fashion design: mansard roofs topped buildings, women donned crinolines, and men grew impressive Napoleon III mustaches. Emulating the Champs-Elysées in Paris, Gilman proposed the broadest and grandest boulevard in America. Its first block, which went up in the 1860s, became home to some of Boston's wealthiest families.

Cross Arlington Street to right side of Comm. Ave.; note house on corner and #5 Comm. Ave.

Montgomery Sears, living at what was then 12 Arlington St., expanded his home into **#1 Comm. Ave. [5],** maintaining the dignity and architectural integrity of Arlington Street, which epitomized the ideals of the Back Bay. He built a glorious second-story music room and hung his growing collection of paintings. The house embodied the lifestyle of the rich and cultured at the end of the 19th century: Paderewski played the piano; Sargent painted the women; the glitterati gathered. By 1925, the mansion had been converted to a convent school, and now it houses elegant condominiums.

Comm. Ave. promenade

Compared to the socially appropriate Sears, non-conformist Walter C. Baylies epitomized the nouveau riche of the Back Bay. He made a fortune in textiles, married well, and mimicked the Brahmin lifestyle, but he could not restrain his desire to literally make his home his castle. Neighbors were appalled when he tore down his 1861 house at **#5 [5],** which was identical to **#3 [5].** He wanted a unique and "befitting" house, not a twin, and his creation was a grand success. The mansion of 1904 includes one of the Back Bay's most extravagant ballrooms, modeled after Le Petit Trianon at Versailles and finished in time for his daughter's debutante ball. The house was always humming with formal parties, musical soirées, the boisterous activities of six children, and the shenanigans of a pet squirrel who subsisted on a diet of brocade draperies.

The Boston Center for Adult Education was housed and offered a variety of courses here until late 2008. It is amusing to visualize aerobics classes in the gilded ballroom where the Baylieses hosted white-tie galas. But after six decades the cost of the real estate became too dear for the nonprofit, and it moved to more practical, albeit less elegant space. The mansion was sold to a family whose children will soon be reinventing the Baylies' lifestyle.

The understated row houses **#20–#36 [6],** built by Gilman and his partner, Gridley J. Fox Bryant, are thought to better represent the architects' conception of the Back Bay than the more exuberant houses across the street. Notable for their shared mansard roof and continu-

Stroll up center of Comm. Ave. Mall; stop at #20

🦶🦶

Continue on mall;
at Berkeley Street,
cross Comm. Ave. to
near-right corner

ity of style, #20–#36 seemingly present a single unit. But upon closer scrutiny, each home reveals subtle differences, making this 175-foot stretch congenial rather than repetitive. The roof is a perfect example of classic mansard: a steep lower portion usually broken by dormer windows and a less angled and shorter upper section. The style is named after its creator, the

#25–#27 Comm. Ave

17th-century French architect François Mansard. The ubiquity of this type of roof in Paris was based on both stylistic and pragmatic rationales: the smaller spaces directly under the mansard were not counted as rooms by the Parisian tax collector.

The tax collector would have capitalized on **#25–#27 [7]**, an extravaganza when built as a free-standing mansion in 1861. The lavish corner garden is still unusual, even in this most up-scale part of town. It was thoughtfully separated from the street by a stone balustrade. Although stately in its day, the wall has started to sag—not surprising for a venerable 150-year-old. Once used by Mass. General Hospital to house families of patients and hospital executives, this mansion has returned to its original role as housing for the financially well endowed, even though the residents are condominium owners, not home owners. There is still cachet in living on the sunny side of Comm. Ave.

Eleven stories of apartment dwellers enjoyed the sunny side in 1894 when **Haddon Hall, #29 Comm. Ave. [8],** was erected as a luxury residential hotel. At the time, buildings were required to be a minimum of three stories high, and so this giant more than met expectations. Although six stories higher than its neighbors, its architectural vocabulary mirrors theirs. Causing an outcry when it was built, its height no longer seems so problematic, both because its style is so simpatico with the neighborhood and because the Boston skyline is filled with many taller buildings.

Turn around to look at #29 Comm. Ave. on corner behind you

First and Second
Church

Walk right on
Berkeley Street
to near corner of
Marlborough and
Berkeley Streets

The visual impact of the **First and Second Church**
[9] is caused by the melding of old and new. The
congregation traces its ancestry to the Puritans.
When they moved to this site in 1867, their church
was designed to be reminiscent of English country
churches. After a devastating fire in 1968, the
building was re-envisioned by architect Paul
Rudolph. His 1971 amalgam incorporates rem-
nants of the wonderful earlier structure to form a

powerful new edifice. The drama is most apparent from Berkeley Street—one can see the sky through the skeleton of the original rose window.

Another juxtaposition is the contrast between the affluence represented by the façades of Back Bay homes and the unadorned alleys running behind the genteel streets. Part of the master plan, they were meant to separate service from society. Peeking down one of these alleys, one can imagine the wagons of tradesmen provisioning at backdoor kitchens.

A rare opportunity to glimpse the lifestyle of the period is offered at the **Gibson House, #137 Beacon Street [10].** Its façade is a twin of the adjacent **#135,** owned by a Gibson cousin. But as in many families, strong facial resemblances may mask very different personalities. It was not atypical in 1860 to build houses as pairs with individualized interiors, and it is said that #135 was by far the more opulent. Interestingly, houses could be personalized through the choice of fixtures and wood trim offered in copiously illustrated catalogs.

To our 21st-century eyes, Victorian life as defined by the Gibson House was, if not opulent, certainly formal and traditional. The highly recommended tour provides an opportunity to experience daily life in the late 19th century and see how technology revolutionized domestic life. As the steam shovel allowed the building of the Back Bay, indoor plumbing, central heating, and gas lighting provided the amenities. But though the house was up-to-date, Mrs. Gibson's grandson (1874–1954) was an anachronism. A committed

Continue on Berkeley Street; peek down Public Alley #421

Turn right onto Beacon Street; walk to #137

Victorian, he maintained the decor and decorum his family had painstakingly created. He was so aware of the house's historical value that by 1936 he entertained his friends only on the stairs. No one was allowed to sit on the furniture, a regulation tempered by Gibson's generous martinis made with his decidedly un-Victorian bathtub gin. A cultivated man with eclectic interests, from horticulture to poetry, he exemplified an era his neighbors had left behind. As they moved to the suburbs, leaving their homes to become dormitories and rooming houses, Gibson donned his full-length fur coat and marched to a different drummer—two blocks to his daily six o'clock dinner at the Ritz.

👣

Turn around and cross Berkeley Street; continue on Beacon Street to #150

Gibson's eccentricities could not compare to those of the outlandish "Mrs. Jack," Isabella Stewart Gardner, a flamboyant émigré from New York. She took Boston by storm when she moved here as a new bride. As a Boston journalist wrote in 1875, "Mrs. Jack Gardner is one of the seven wonders of Boston. There is nobody like her in any city in this country . . . All Boston is divided into two parts, one of which follows science, and the other Mrs. Jack Gardner." Her idiosyncrasies were legendary—from her afternoon walks, strolling with her leashed pet lion, to her formal soirées, sporting butterfly antennae topped with diamonds. Her house, an 1861 wedding gift from papa, stood at **#150–#152 Beacon Street [11]**. The Gardner home was replaced in 1904, but here on Beacon Street Mrs. Jack started amassing what would become a world-famous art collection. It included her portrait by John Singer Sargent, which seems gracious and genteel by today's standards but was considered risqué at the time. Her décolleté and sumptuous belt of pearls so scandalized society that her husband withdrew the canvas from public view. The painting now hangs in the Isabella Stewart Gardner Museum, a highly recommended visit (see Indoor Footnotes).

Jack Gardner died in 1898. Isabella dealt with her grief by touring the world and accumulating more great works of art. She left Beacon Street three and a half years later. The number 152 was retired at her request—a memory of a bygone era. Her new residence, a palazzo on the Fenway, was designed as a museum in which she could share her art with *tout* Boston while living sumptuously on the upper level. Invitations to her parties were, as always, coveted; for as horrified as Brahmin society was at her exhibitionism, no one would be caught dead missing a Mrs. Jack event.

Like Mrs. Jack, the 1965 anomaly at **#180 Beacon Street [12]** flouts conformity. According to the American Institute of Architects, "all of the design standards established by the Back Bay's fine Victorian architecture were violated with this building's height, bulk and extensive use of metal and glass . . . It is one of the buildings that sounded the alarm and helped reinforce the preservation of historic Back Bay architecture."

Even in the heartland of Victoriana, however, it is hard to ignore contemporary architecture. Walking across Clarendon Street, one is struck by the magnificent Hancock Tower, visible from many places in the city, but particularly dramatic from this vantage point. Architectural critic Donlyn

Turn left onto
Clarendon Street

Lyndon summarizes its omnipresence: "It may be nihilistic, overbearing, even elegantly rude, but it's not dull . . . It is brilliantly packaged, its surface smoothly reflecting the changing character of the sky. It is a landmark worth looking at, even when you shouldn't have to."

This 60-story rhomboid, 740 feet high, presents different faces, depending on the color of the sky and the angle from which you view it. Its profiles will present themselves as you approach the building; the excitement of seeing the complete structure at Copley Square is part of the finale of this walk.

‼
Stop mid-mall on
Clarendon Street

Whereas Arthur Gilman was the visionary responsible for both the concept and much of the building of the Back Bay, Henry Hobson Richardson is the architect whose name is the most well known. His gem, Trinity Church, the area's most extraordinary building, will also be visited at the end of this walk. Here is the architect's trial run, the 1872 **First Baptist (Brattle Square) Church [13],** a handsome puddingstone edifice, most admired for its Florentine-style tower.

Richardson was young, only 31 years old, when he received this commission. His youth and inexperience resulted in a building noteworthy for its terrible acoustics and a huge cost overrun. But he did recognize some of his limitations and hired sculptor Frédéric-Auguste Bartholdi to create the tower frieze. (Bartholdi would later sculpt New York's Statue of Liberty, which almost became Boston's Statue of Liberty. When New Yorkers were reluctant to pay for the base, Bartholdi offered the statue to his friend Richardson in Boston; New Yorkers quickly reconsidered.) The frieze depicts four of the sacraments: baptism, communion, marriage, and death. The faces carved in relief were not divine imaginings, however, but rather the likenesses of contemporary Bostonians, including Longfellow, Emerson, and Hawthorne. Yet the celebrities with whom the church is most associated are the trumpeting angels who gild each corner of the tower and give the building its affectionate nickname, the "Church of the Holy Beanblowers."

Turn right; continue walking up center of mall; stop across from #121 Comm. Ave.

A delightful confection, **#121 Comm. Ave. [14]** is an 1872 Ruskinian Gothic. This architectural style, named after English art critic John Ruskin, is characterized by detailed ornamentation, natural hues, and dynamism. Color was used profusely. Embellishment was lavish. Mass production of ornamentation ensured its availability. It was said that the Victorians dreaded simplicity—certainly Ruskinian Gothic was not dull. "The entire vision valued architecture as an embodiment of human emotion." Popular in England in the 1860s, it flourished in the United States in the 1870s. This whimsical house, with its multicolored building materials—wrought iron, slate, stone, wood, and brick—is a paradigm of Ruskin's ideal.

#128 and **#130 Comm. Ave. [15]** represent the baroque ideal that held currency at the turn of the century at the Ecole des Beaux-Arts in Paris. Originally red brick, these fashionable dowagers were gussied up in 1905. They get their extravagant personalities from the carved stone instead of a pastiche of colors and materials. There are very few representatives of this sumptuous style in conservative Boston; many observers have noted these buildings would seem more at home on New York's Fifth Avenue.

Not so the ladies of the quietly prominent **Chilton Club** on the corner at **#152 Comm. Ave. [16].** Architecturally, their club is unremarkable but for the exclusivity implied by its three entrances: the front door for members, the side door for members accompanying guests, and the alley entrance for servants and tradesmen. Founded as a sewing club in 1910 and named after Mary Chilton, the first female Pilgrim to set foot on Plymouth Rock, this institution was for many years considered the female counterpart to the elite Somerset Club (See Beacon Hill Walk). Historically, members were known for their charitable works, gardening, cultural interests, and debutante balls; they were identified by their "sensible coats, sensible shoes and sensible hats." An apocryphal tale: not so long ago, a transplanted New Yorker complimented one of the ladies on her hat and asked where she got it. The hat wearer replied, "My dear, we don't *get* our hats, we *have* our hats!"

👣

Stop at sculpture on mall at near side of Dartmouth Street; look diagonally across left side of Comm. Ave. at gray limestone Hotel Vendome

This **black granite sculpture [17]** is Boston's understated, eloquent memorial to the nine firefighters who died in the great **Hotel Vendome [18]** fire of 1972. It stands in stark contrast to the building they tried to save. The 100-year-old building has had three architects, three incarnations, and now as office and condo space it seems a disjointed combination of unsympathetic styles and additions. Yet in its heyday, this was the grande dame of Boston hospitality—each room accessorized with fireplace, private bathroom, and steam heat. She was radiant, both literally, as the first commercial building in the city to have electricity, and figuratively, with an illustrious guest list that included artists, diplomats, patricians, and presidents.

The **Ames-Webster House** at **#306 Dartmouth Street [19]** competed for distinction with the Hotel Vendome. By 1872, when it was erected, Back Bay residents were less intimidated by architectural convention and more disposed to flaunt their individuality and wealth. The house assimilated all the exciting architectural features of the era: mansard roofs, dormer windows, stained glass, and multiple building materials. But the highlight, added in 1882, was a porte-cochère on the Dartmouth Street side; unfortunately, it has been transmogrified into an enclosed archway. Male guests entered through a doorway to the first floor; the women alighted under the porte-cochère, took an elevator to the second floor, powdered their noses, and made a grand entrance down the majestic interior staircase.

Across Dartmouth Street, the **Hollis H. Hunnewell House** at **#315 [20],** built seven years later, clearly enjoyed "mansard envy." This flamboyant mansion vied to be the showplace of the neighborhood. It had *everything:* mansards, chimneys, dormers, towers, trims, tiles, pilasters, paneling, and fine brickwork. Remarkably, this jumble is a success rather than a caricature.

Two 1870s dwellings that make a good "contrast and compare" exercise are the **Cushing-Endicott**

Walk right on
Dartmouth Street

Turn left onto
Marlborough Street

House at **#163–#165 Marlborough Street** and the **Crowninshield House** at **#164 [21].** The eminent architectural scholar Bainbridge Bunting refers to the former as "perhaps the handsomest house in the whole Back Bay." And yet this restrained and balanced composition was created by architects of little renown. Interestingly, the Crowninshield House, designed by revered architect H. H. Richardson, is considered a learning experience. Although there are some glimmers of his future creativity in the decorative ceramic tile and brickwork, the whole adds up to far less than the sum of its parts.

! !

Continue to
Fairfield Street

The grace of the next one and a half blocks of **Marlborough Street** is indeed more than the sum of its parts. Cozy, understated, and intimate, this area has more 19th-century atmosphere than the neighboring streets. In spring, the overhanging trees and fanciful gardens soften the cityscape and further enhance the street's unpretentious character. But Back Bay was not always as green. In fact, at first trees were planned only for the Comm. Ave. Mall and did not appear elsewhere until the 20th century. Early Back Bay residents did not bother with foliage since they usually summered outside Boston and considered their city homes merely pieds-à-terre for the winter social season. Stroll this quiet residential path, heed the roiling brick sidewalks (especially mountainous after winter frost heaves), and particularly note the following houses. **Number 191 [22]** is considered an archetype of Ruskinian Gothic style and is exceptional because of its oversized entrance portico with a striking iron grille. **Number 196 [22]** is described by architectural critic Donlyn Lyndon as "great entertainment from top to bottom." Look for the whimsical eyebrow dormer.

Notice the common theme of bay windows. "The look" originated in Regency England (1811–1820) and was consummately used by Charles Bulfinch in Boston (see Beacon Hill Walk). Nevertheless, when they appeared mechanically on every new home without regard to the integrity of the structure, not everyone was a fan. Henry James referred to the style as "detested vitreous." Here, however, one can imagine the play of light enlivening the interior spaces and can appreciate the interest and drama added to the exterior façade.

The Queen Anne houses that line fair **Fairfield Street [23]** are colorful, unpretentious, and detailed; they represent an emphasis on quality craftsmanship. Their charm is revealed in subtleties rather than massive scale. This English style began to flourish here in the late 1870s. The dud of the block is **#21.** Widely assumed to be a poor copy of H. H. Richardson's work, it is, according to Bainbridge Bunting, "a welter of competing forms—complete artistic indigestion. This is a typical instance of the way H. H. Richardson's contemporaries misunderstood and misused his style of architecture." The *AIA Guide to Boston* completes the analysis, "The fenestration is disorderly . . . and the ornamentation has gotten out of hand."

But one thing that always remained orderly in Victorian Boston was social stratification. As New Yorkers George and Ira Gershwin wryly observed in their little-known 1946 ditty, "The

Turn left onto
Fairfield Street

Back Bay Polka," the same standards were upheld into the 20th century:

Keep up the cultured pose
By looking down your nose;
Keep up the status quos—Or they'll keep you out
of Boston.
At natural history we are colossal;
That is because, you see,
At first hand we study the fossil.
Strangers are all dismissed—(Not that we're
prejudiced)
You simply don't exist—if you haven't been born
in Boston . . .
You're of the bourgeoisie,
And no one bothers—Not if your family tree
Doesn't date from the Pilgrim Fathers.
Therefore, when all is said,
Life is so limit-ed,
You find, unless you're dead,
You never get ahead in Boston.
You never get ahead,
Unless you're dead—You never get ahead in
Boston.

According to Cleveland Amory, himself an insider and astute observer of this social class, a proper Bostonian so identifies with his ancestors that when he is asked, "How long have you been in Boston?" his automatic response is "Since 1730," and he really believes it. The two key branches of his romanticized family tree include an 18th-century sea captain and a 19th-century capitalist. One created the mystique, the other the means to live it.

‼

Turn left onto Comm. Ave.; walk down center of mall; stop across from #217 Comm. Ave.

Many of the "true" Bostonians of whom the Gershwins sang belonged to this block's **Algonquin Club** at **#217 Comm. Ave.** or the **St. Botolph Club** at **#199 [24].** The former was established in 1885 as a place for Brahmins to transact business, discreetly. Its façade, however, is anything but quiet, decorated with pilasters, carvings, and a variety of windows and balconies. Designed by Stanford White, of the renowned New York architectural firm McKim, Mead and White, this opulent Italian Renaissance mansion violated the city's stringent building codes by protruding beyond the allowable setback. Despite its influential membership, the Algonquin was forced to rebuild. Today, the membership reflects a more diverse "who's who" in Boston, having admitted women and African Americans in the 1980s.

Reflecting the intellectual life of the city, the St. Botolph Club was founded in 1880 by artists, writers, musicians, and their patrons. It sponsored the first exhibition in this country of both Monet and John Singer Sargent. It was at St. Botolph that Sargent's scandalous portrait of Isabella Stewart Gardner was unveiled, and it was from St. Botolph that Jack Gardner removed it. The club moved to this address in 1972, converting the building from a private home. Interestingly, the home was built by McKim, Mead and White only three years after their grandly designed Algonquin Club. This style harkens back to another era; it is Boston in 1800, a Federal Revival building more understated than glamorous. Critic Donlyn Lyndon observes:

*Back Bay in Beacon Hill dress, tailored so well
that you hardly notice . . . but the game here was
to make personal decision unnecessary or at least
invisible, by adopting the decorous garb of an earlier era . . . This is one of the first buildings to result from a serious and self-conscious look at
Boston's own Classical architecture as a source of
inspiration . . . The whole is handsomely sedate.*

Stop at statue of
Samuel Eliot
Morison on near
side of mall at
Exeter Street

Patrician Samuel Eliot Morison was the quintessential St. Botolph member: Beacon Hill childhood, revered Harvard professor, avid sailor, author
of 48 books, and two-time Pulitzer Prize winner.
His statue is probably the most well known and
emotionally approachable on the Comm. Ave.
Mall, depicting a man in an environment he loved.

Staying on mall,
cross Exeter Street;
stop across from
#191 Comm. Ave.

At **#191 Comm. Ave.** stands the **Hotel Agassiz
[25],** as prominent for its residents as for its style.
Built in 1872 by Henry Lee Higginson, one of
the richest men in Boston, and named for his
wife, Ida Agassiz, it was communal living at its
best. One of the few luxury multifamily dwellings
in the Back Bay, each of its six floors contained a
single floor-through unit; yet the building itself
was unpretentious, as was Higginson. Conversely,
his philanthropy was extraordinary. He founded
the Boston Symphony Orchestra and for many
years was its primary benefactor. He modeled his
life on an adage he took from the duke of Devonshire: "What I gave, I have; what I spent, I had;
what I kept, I lost."

A treasured gift is a stroll on this part of Comm.
Ave. during the brief period in which the magnolias are in bloom. Although these spectacular

trees are fixtures of many Back Bay gardens, the sheer number on this stretch of the avenue intensifies the beauty. All seasons have their charm, but many locals especially appreciate the magnolias in this city where winter is long and gray. Their April flowering defines spring.

Charming in all seasons is William Ralph Emerson's Queen Anne delight, the former **Boston Art Club** at **#270 Dartmouth Street [26]**. Its oversized arch, elaborate carving, and fantastical silhouette made it a Victorian crowd-pleaser. The club was conveniently located for Boston's art enthusiasts who patronized the new Museum of Fine Arts, then situated in nearby Copley Square. Boston has preserved this fine building by converting it to a public high school.

The assemblage of buildings before you constitutes Boston's famous **Copley Square.** As observed by *Boston Ways* author George F. Weston Jr., "Copley Square . . . is a rare jewel on the variegated tapestry that is Boston. Architecturally one of the most interesting as well as one of the most attractive squares in America, Copley blends six utterly different types of architecture into a composite whole which is delightfully pleasing. Why this should be so is a problem for architects and artists, but it is the fact." Another extraordinary fact is that this landmark was transformed from a particularly dirty, dusty, and undesirable piece of landfill that abutted the railroad tracks.

One hundred years ago all that a cultured Brahmin needed was here: Trinity Church for the soul, the Boston Public Library for the mind,

Continue on Comm. Ave. Mall; turn right onto Dartmouth Street

Cross Boylston Street to steps of Boston Public Library

and the Museum of Fine Arts for aesthetic enlightenment. While Bostonians will not find all those needs met in Copley Square today, the area provides other opportunities: summertime concerts, a farmers' market, restaurants, and lots of shopping.

❗❗

Look back at church at corner of Boylston and Dartmouth Streets

Tucked in the corner of monumental Copley Square, the **New Old South Church [27]** may be too upstaged by its neighbors to be fully appreciated. Its Ruskinian Gothic glory is manifested by its multicolored and patterned stonework and Italianate tower. The campanile, still eye-catching, was once quite a bit higher. But almost from the start it began to tilt. This "leaning tower of Boston" became the object of much speculation and wagering: when would it fall and on whom? By 1931, it was listing so dangerously, already 3 feet out of plumb, that it was taken down stone by stone, reinforced, and built back up again, though not quite as high as the 1875 original. This former Puritan congregation is known today for its liberal bias and open-minded inclusivity—a far cry from its early days when parishioner John Alden was sentenced to 15 weeks in jail for witchcraft.

The smooth granite **Boston Public Library (BPL) [28]** stands in stately contrast to the picturesque New Old South Church. The BPL's mandate, to be "a palace for the people," reflects the belief that every citizen can benefit from great literature, art, and science. Accessibility was the underlying vision—patrons would, for the first time, be able to borrow books, and branch libraries would bring knowledge to the neighborhoods.

Widely acclaimed as a splendid Renaissance Revival, the first of its style in America, the BPL was designed by Charles McKim of McKim, Mead and White, the same firm that designed the Algonquin and St. Botolph clubs. While Henry James spoke for those who thought it a brilliant classical structure, calling it "a Florentine palace magnificently superseding all others," it had its detractors as well—*The Boston Globe* compared it to the city morgue. Completed in 1895, it took seven years to build, at a cost of $2.5 million, a mere five times the budget. Yet for his seven years of work, McKim, who raised much of the money himself, garnered only $22,000 in fees. Perhaps in lieu of payment, he tried to immortalize his firm's illustrious name by cleverly disguising it among the catalog of greats adorning the panels of the parapet. Once a local newspaper uncovered this secret, the architect was pressured to remove his shot at posterity.

McKim brought to his design team a roster of 19th-century luminaries in the arts. Approaching the library entrance, one is struck by Bela Pratt's monumental seated statues. On the right, Art holds her palette, symbol of her vocation; on the left, her counterpart, Science, contemplates the mysteries of the world. The grand doors just inside the main entrance, created by the sculptor Daniel Chester French, represent (from left to right) Music and Poetry; Knowledge and Wisdom; Truth and Romance. The rather cold gray and black exterior stands in marked contrast to the warm tones that envelop you upon entering the vaulted lobby. *Boston Ways* author George F. Weston, Jr., observed,

"The interior of the building is illuminated like a medieval missal."

Climb the impressive marble staircase, passing Louis Saint-Gaudens's literary lions, to the loggia on the second level. The scenes painted here, by France's great muralist Pierre Puvis de Chavannes, were meant to symbolize the wealth of knowledge collected in the BPL. Decipher the 19th-century clues to identify the lovely ladies' specialties. To the left and right of the windows are Chemistry and Physics; the right staircase wall represents Pastoral, Epic, and Dramatic Poetry; the left wall signifies History, Astronomy, and Philosophy. And straight ahead is *The Muses of Inspiration Welcoming the Harbinger of Light*—not exactly a paean to feminism. Note the muses fawning over the naked young man. Yet an oblique tribute to women can be found in the Elliot Room to the left of the second-floor landing. Whereas the frieze on the "Church of the Holy Beanblowers" paid homage to the intellectual male icons of the day, here *The Triumph of Time* ceiling figures were modeled after Boston's female social lights. As one wit observed, "See that lantern jaw? I bet she's a Saltonstall."

Other rooms worth a visit are the Bates Room straight ahead, with its period furnishings; the Delivery Room to the right, with its mural *The Quest of the Holy Grail* by Edwin Austin Abbey; and the third-floor lobby, with John Singer Sargent's murals entitled *The Triumph of Religion*, his 30-year opus. This latter work was highly controversial in its day, for Judaism was depicted as "a

If you wish to explore the BPL's interior, walk upstairs to second floor. If you are pressed for time, skip the next 3 paragraphs and proceed to the next direction.

wounded suffering being, in contrast to the triumphant pose of Christianity."

As you leave the library, look through the landing windows into the charming central courtyard, home of the scandalously controversial (she was actually "banned in Boston") Bacchante. McKim donated Frederick MacMonnies's statue to the BPL, and Boston reacted with puritanical panic. After all, this was a *naked* woman, holding her *naked* child in one arm and *intoxicating grapes* in the other. The trustees hardly considered this statue appropriate to their mission of educating the masses. An irritated McKim withdrew the statue and sent it to the more open-minded Metropolitan Museum of Art in New York. Fortunately, MacMonnies made a second casting of the beautiful Bacchante. Boston came to its senses and she now resides in the Boston Museum of Fine Arts; the one before you in the BPL is a contemporary copy.

Here you get a glimpse of why the BPL has been dubbed by some as "Beauty and the Beast." The contemporary "Beast" is Philip Johnson's 1972 functional addition, which provides modern conveniences and space that were missing in McKim's "Beauty." But the real fairy tale is the story of how the new building was underwritten. John Defarrai, an impoverished Italian immigrant, began his career as a street vendor. He used the BPL resources to study finance and subsequently made a fortune in stocks, bonds, and real estate. Notwithstanding, he always lived modestly in a rented room that cost $8.50 a week. When he died in 1950, he bequeathed multimillion-

Leave BPL; walk back to Boylston Street; turn left; walk toward new addition to BPL

dollar gifts to the library and other Boston institutions to thank the city that allowed him to become so successful.

❗❗
Return to center of
Copley Square; face
hotel on your right

Here stood the original Museum of Fine Arts, whose collection outgrew its space. In 1909 when it moved a mile west to the more spacious area on the Fenway (see Indoor Foot Notes) it was replaced by the aristocratic **Copley Plaza Hotel [29].** Although the building is not as architecturally stellar as its neighbors, it is a very pleasing edifice that graciously accommodated the great balls and cotillions of a bygone era. New Yorkers and Washingtonians may recognize its siblings, the Plaza Hotel and the Willard Hotel, respectively—the father of all three was architect Henry Hardenberg.

❗❗
Continue to front of
Hancock Tower

In contrast to the hotel, the **John Hancock Tower** (1968–76) **[30]** was considered one of the most exciting and problematic constructions in New England. The gestation was particularly long, the birth was particularly complicated, but the baby is now healthy and thriving. Henry N. Cobb, supervising architect from the firm of I. M. Pei & Partners, hoped to deflect concerns about overshadowing Trinity Church by reflecting its glory. The tower does so magnificently, in large part due to its huge windowpanes and the angle at which the building is sited.

As Mark Feeney observed in *The Boston Globe*, "When Hancock announced the project, criticism was swift, vocal, and widespread. The Boston Society of Architects called it 'an egotistical monument.'" The political tenor of the 1960s found everything the building represented to be anathema; large corporate statements were out of style. Political activist Abbie Hoffman stood with his followers on the library steps, gestured emphatically at the construction site, and ranted, "There is the enemy." Less than 15 years later, the building was honored by both the American Institute of Architects and the very same Boston Society of Architects that had so scathingly maligned it. The latter declared, "The Committee has no doubts that the tower is the most beautiful contemporary tower in Boston, and probably in the entire United States."

But the windowpanes, an essential part of the design, refused to stay in place. They began to fly off the building, much to the dismay of passers-by on the street below. Eventually all were replaced by more secure installations. But for those inside the building, life was still unsettling. An unlikely malady for workers in a skyscraper is motion sickness—but indeed, woozy they were, for the tower swayed in the wind. To counter the building's instability, a balancing contraption was installed on the 58th floor: a Rube Goldberg–like combination of 300-ton sliding lead weights, steel plates, shock absorbers, and springs. Yet fear persisted that, under certain conditions, the tall, slender building would be vulnerable to toppling winds— hence, 1,500 tons of steel bracing now reinforce the entire structure.

Once the Hancock was secured, Trinity Church had to be reinforced as well, for as the Hancock went up, Trinity settled. The church is supported by a system of wooden pilings that work only if submerged in the water under the landfill. As the Hancock was stabilized, the pilings were found to be high and dry, threatening the church with collapse. The Hancock Insurance Company had to pull out its own policies to pay for the installation of pumps to regulate the water level below Trinity. Paradoxically, despite all the modern technology that saved both buildings, for many years a simple rowboat monitored the health of the support system—as long as it stayed afloat in the water beneath the church basement, so would the church.

‼️
Return to center of Copley Square, facing church

Trinity Church [31], the focal point of Copley Square, is consistently counted among America's top ten most beautiful buildings by the American Institute of Architects. One's initial impression of balance, harmony, and majesty is enhanced by closer scrutiny of both the exterior and interior. This magnificent edifice was the vision of two brilliant men, the enterprising minister of the church, Phillips Brooks, and the innovative architect, H. H. Richardson.

The original Trinity Church was located downtown. It fell to the deadly fire of 1872, which destroyed much of that neighborhood. Although the fire was the immediate catalyst, the congregation was already planning to leave the commercial district. In anticipation of this move they had purchased land in the up-and-coming Back Bay. Brooks was anxious to lead the charge and was hugely influential in choosing H. H. Richardson as architect of the new church building. Richardson was only 34 years old, lived in New York, and had neither the reputation nor the experience of

Trinity Church

the other architects competing for the commission. Some say his success was based on his design of the "Beanblowers" church tower; more say it was based on his social designs—for many on the church building committee were his old Harvard classmates and fellow members of the exclusive Porcellian Club (see Cambridge Walk). Nonetheless, his cronyism was our good fortune, for Trinity is a building that is egalitarian in its appeal, despite its exclusive conception.

The realization of the design, however, was a collective phenomenon. As described by English writer Paul Hogarth, it was "a cultural event of great importance, bringing together on a medieval scale architects, painters, and craftsmen to create one of the most sumptuously satisfying religious buildings of the 19th century."

Vitally American, but with French lineage, Trinity was inspired by 11th-century churches in southwestern France. Though Gothic style was the Victorian ideal, Richardson felt that the less ethereal, more robust Romanesque style better reflected the American character. There is a consensus among architectural critics that the church's vitality is attributable to the tension between the density of the building and the energy and joyfulness of the design elements. The colonnades march up the façade, while the horizontal bands of red sandstone anchor the rough granite. The irregularly hewn stone, massive sturdy tower, and imaginative mixture of materials, colors, and patterns came to be known as Richardsonian Romanesque and opened a wonderfully inventive new chapter in American architecture. Here is the irrepressible spirit of the nation, firmly planted on the ground by the somber colors of the porch and rising, rough and tumble, to the optimistic red tiles of the tower.

The ingenuity of the design is matched by the brilliance of the engineering that allows this massive structure to stand on land with such a high water table. It is supported by 4,500 wooden pilings driven through 30 feet of gravel fill—2,000 of these for the 11-million-pound tower alone. Today, the church has successfully completed a 21st-century engineering challenge: the basement, which until recently was little more than a crawl space, had its floor lowered to accommodate full-height meeting rooms and a new book and gift shop. High-tech pumps removed the underlying water without disturbing the foundations, which are gloriously revealed in the new undercroft. The *Boston Globe* elaborates: "A delicate tracery of wood spans the new space, giving it the feel of a garden house, while art-glass doors and partitions . . . are as delicate as a watercolor wash of distant scenery."

Walk around left side of church to the cloister

Walking outside the building, you immediately encounter the impressive statue of the indomitable Reverend Brooks, a sculpture befitting a man larger than life. At his shoulder stands Christ, inspiring Brooks as he preaches. This 1907 work by Augustus Saint-Gaudens is a fitting tribute to the man so responsible for the creation of Trinity Church. And the inscription on its base is a remarkably simple epitaph that calls to mind the Gershwins' witty observation about what is truly important to Bostonians:

> *Preacher of the Word of God*
> *Lover of all Mankind*
> *Born in Boston*
> *Died in Boston*

Although most visitors are drawn to the front façade of the church, the delicacy of the adjoining parish house and cloister is further testament to

Richardson's vision. Donlyn Lyndon's description captures its essence: "In what is surely one of the smoothest, most carefree gestures in American architecture, the cloister colonnade simply steps up the side of the parish house and merges with the mass. In this spot alone H. H. Richardson epitomizes the characteristic that makes his buildings live where others are inert." Furthermore, Lyndon admonishes, "If you're planning to dash in and out, don't. It's a waste of the serenity of the place. This is one of the few places in America where a full range of talent in the visual arts can be seen at work, and here the creative capacity is writ large."

Enter and tour church

As you buy your tickets, be sure to pick up the informative self-guided tour of the church interior. (Trinity also offers frequent docent-led tours.) The first impression upon entering the church combines intimacy with awe, and the man who successfully reconciled these disparate sentiments was John La Farge. He was responsible for the interior design, he created much of the magnificent stained-glass and mural work himself, and he hired the best artisans and artists of the era, including the young Augustus Saint-Gaudens, William Morris, and Edward Burne-Jones. Astonishingly, this work was all accomplished in just five months and finished a mere eight days before the church was consecrated on February 9, 1877. Brooks's mandate to La Farge was that he "put something up there that will be an inspiration to me as I stand in the pulpit to preach." Indeed, he did.

The red-, green-, and gold-hued walls warmly embrace the stained-glass windows and the mural cycle along the chancel wall. But perhaps La Farge's most inspirational work in the entire church is *Christ in Majesty,* a brilliant blue-glass window over the entrance. It is constructed of countless small opalescent roundels. La Farge invented and employed a new technique called plating, in which glass is arranged in layers, allowing for subtle shading and depth of color. (This style would be used later by his famous student Louis Comfort Tiffany.) One can imagine Brooks's impassioned orations from his pulpit, inspired by the light shining through La Farge's stained glass. His cascading words, once clocked at an astonishing 213 per minute, carried throughout the church; its wonderful acoustics derive from the Greek-cross shape of the building and its hanging barrel vaulting.

Yet Brooks, for all his majesty, requested that the chancel and its furnishings reflect what he considered "the two great functions of the church: the central role of preaching and Holy Eucharist celebrated at a simple table." The chancel in Brooks's time stood in marked contrast to what one sees now. It was "reminiscent of the early Christian church. Richardson designed an open space with a wooden rail and communion table. There was no cross or altar." Today's marble and gold are 20th-century adornments.

As Brooks felt the chancel should be simple, he likewise felt the church should be open to all. He insisted that gallery seating be available in addition to the traditional privately owned pews. By the 1940s the practice of pew ownership had been abandoned; yet the custom of parishioners needlepointing kneeling benches continues—a homey touch in this soaring ecclesiastical masterpiece.

Stop at small statue of Tortoise and Hare in front of fountain at left of Trinity Church

From the soul to the sole . . . this walk ends where Boston Marathoners do. The famous 26.2-mile race, America's first marathon, began in 1897 with only 16 contestants. Today approximately 25,000 people compete and then converge, celebrate, and collapse in Copley Square after running the grueling course. And Nancy Schon's **statue of the Tortoise and the Hare [32]** represents two ways of running a marathon and two ways of approaching Newbury Street, Boston's upscale shopping district. One hundred and fifty years ago, it was for people who had neither purse nor prominence—how things have changed. For shopping, eating, or people watching, Newbury Street is one of Boston's best choices.

Beacon Hill

"The sunny street that holds the sifted few."
—Oliver Wendell Holmes

Essential Information for Walk Two

Length of walk:	1 ³⁄₄ miles
Terrain:	hilly
Time:	2 ¹⁄₄ hours at a leisurely pace, without going inside any of the buildings
Nearest T stop:	Charles Street/MGH on Red Line
Starting point:	Exit T and walk up left side of Cambridge Street for 3 ¹⁄₂ blocks to Harrison Gray Otis House, 141 Cambridge Street

Supplements to the Walk

Highly Recommended

Guided tour of Harrison Gray Otis House

Time:	45 minutes
Hours:	Wed.–Sun., 11:00 A.M.–4:30 P.M.
	every half-hour
Telephone:	617-227-3957
Admission:	$8; $24 maximum per family
When:	at start of walk at
	141 Cambridge Street

Visit Museum of African American History

Time:	35 minutes
Hours:	Mon.–Sat., 10:00 A.M.–4:00 P.M.
Telephone:	617-725-0022
Admission:	free; suggested donation $5
When:	first third of walk at
	46 Joy Street

Browse and lunch on Charles Street; explore the Flats, the Victorian neighborhood west of Charles Street

When:	end of walk

Of Further Interest

Guided tour of Nichols House Museum

Time:	30 minutes
Hours:	Apr.–Oct.: Tues.–Sat., 11:00 A.M.–
	4:00 P.M., every half-hour
Telephone:	617-227-6993
Admission:	$7; children free
When:	second third of walk at
	55 Mount Vernon Street

Guided tour of third Harrison Gray Otis House

Time: 30 minutes
Hours: Mon.–Fri., no set tours
                 scheduled; call in advance
                 to arrange
Telephone: 617-227-2425
Admission: free
When: last third of walk, American
                 Meteorological Society at
                 45 Beacon Street

Guided tour of State House

Time: 40 minutes
Hours: Mon.–Sat., schedule varies; call
                 in advance
Telephone: 617-727-3676
Admission: free
When: last third of walk at
                 top of Beacon Street

Guided tour of Black Heritage Trail

Time: 2 hours
Hours: Memorial Day–Labor Day:
                 daily, 10:00 A.M., 12:00 and
                 2:00 P.M.; other months: call to
                 reserve
Telephone: 617-742-5415
Admission: free
When: end of walk; leaves from Shaw
                 Memorial at top of Beacon Street

Beacon Hill - Walk Two

1. Harrison Gray Otis House
2. #74 Joy Street
3. Smith Court
4. African Meeting House
5. Holmes Alley
6. #5 Pinckney Street
7. #20 Pinckney Street
8. #24 Pinckney Street
9. Site of former Phillips School
10. #62 Pinckney Street
11. #74 ½ Pinckney Street
12. #85 Pinckney Street
13. Louisburg Square
14. #20 Louisburg Square
15. #13–#19 Louisburg Square
16. #86 Pinckney Street
17. #40 West Cedar Street
18. #9 West Cedar Street
19. Acorn Street
20. Harvard Musical Association
21. #29A Chestnut Street
22. #27 Chestnut Street
23. #17, #15, and #13 Chestnut Street
24. #8 Walnut Street
25. #14 Walnut Street
26. #55 and #57 Mount Vernon Street
27. #59–#83 Mount Vernon Street
28. #50–#60 Mount Vernon Street
29. Charles Street Meeting House
30. Former site of Blaxton house
31. #33–#45 Beacon Street
32. State House
33. Major General "Fighting Joe" Hooker
34. Shaw Memorial
35. Boston Common
36. Park Street T Station

Beacon Hill

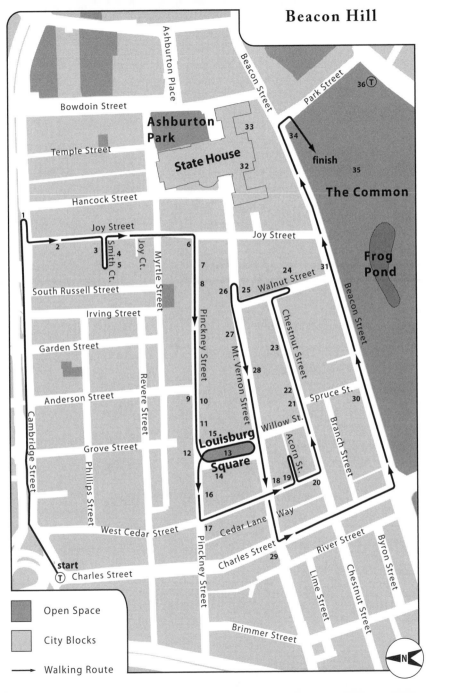

Ashburton Place

Bowdoin Street

Temple Street

Ashburton Park

State House

33

32

Hancock Street

Beacon Street

Park Street

36 Ⓣ

34

finish

35

The Common

1

Joy Street

2

3

Smith Ct.

4

5

Joy Ct.

Myrtle Street

6

Joy Street

South Russell Street

Irving Street

Garden Street

Revere Street

Anderson Street

Pinckney Street

7

8

26 25

Walnut Street

24

31

27

Chestnut Street

23

28

Frog Pond

9 10

Mt. Vernon Street

22

21

Spruce St.

30

11

15

Louisburg

13

Square

14

12

Willow St.

Acorn St.

18 19

20

Branch Street

Beacon Street

Grove Street

16

17

Cedar Lane Way

Phillips Street

West Cedar Street

Pinckney Street

Charles Street

29

River Street

Lime Street

Chestnut Street

Byron Street

Cambridge Street

start

Ⓣ Charles Street

Brimmer Street

Open Space

City Blocks

→ Walking Route

Ⓝ

> **This is good old Boston**
> **The home of the bean and the cod**
> **Where the Lowells talk to the Cabots**
> **And the Cabots talk only to God**
> —Dr. John Collins Bossidy, 1910

Stand in front of
141 Cambridge
Street, Otis House
Museum

It is likely you have heard of Boston's First Families, the Lowells and the Cabots, but you may never have encountered Harrison Gray Otis. Yet it was Otis who gave birth to this city's patrician neighborhood on Beacon Hill. Unfortunately for young Harry, his father, although well born and a great patriot, lost all his money in the Revolutionary War. Armed only with the right pedigree, Otis became a successful lawyer and politician, eventually holding office in both Boston and Washington—all the while amassing a fortune in real estate and business ventures. Ambitious, smart, and entrepreneurial, he may have been the original yuppie.

Otis's first house is the only surviving 18th-century mansion in the city, a lone reminder of a once fashionable residential neighborhood. In 1795 he commissioned Charles Bulfinch, a young architect, to design this house for his growing family. It was the first of three houses that Bulfinch would plan for Otis in the following ten years.

Bulfinch was the foremost architect in Boston in the decades following the Revolution. A contemporary of Otis, he grew up in a wealthy Boston family, attended Harvard, and lived the life of an aesthete. He spent two years on the grand tour of Europe, returning home with great admiration for English architecture. The next several years were, in his own words, "a season of leisure, pursuing no business, but giving gratuitous advice in architecture." Despite this self-deprecating assessment, Bulfinch was to change the face of Boston. From 1788 to 1818 (when he left at President Monroe's behest to become the architect of the United States Capitol) he designed three state capitols, three churches, two public monuments, schools, office buildings, banks, a theater, a concert hall, hospitals, three entire streets, and numerous private houses. Most of what remains you will see on this walk.

As you stand in front of the house, notice the following architectural features, the kernels of Bulfinch's Federal style: a flat and symmetrical façade, string courses (horizontal lines of stone) that define each story, keystones above the windows, beautiful fanlights, and simple columns on either side of a recessed and elegant entryway. This style would grow to incorporate more elements in Bulfinch's later houses, but the core is evident here. However, the house has not always looked this pristine; prior to restoration, the exterior of the house reflected its use as a ladies' Turkish bath, a patent medicine shop, and a boardinghouse.

To ground you in the history of Beacon Hill, we recommend taking a tour of the **Harrison Gray Otis House [1].** Beautifully refurbished, it affords the opportunity to glimpse life within a wealthy young family's home at the turn of the 18th century—for Otis was only 30 years old when he commissioned the house. When it was first opened to the public, the interior replicated the colonial Williamsburg style: subdued, almost drab. After chemical analysis and further research, curators realized the original decor was brighter—in fact, rather flamboyant. The knowledgeable guides provide a delightful 45-minute talk about both the house and its occupants.

!!
Cross Cambridge Street; walk one block right to Joy Street

Cambridge Street was once the border of Otis's elite residential neighborhood. During the same era, this area at the base of the hill was not at all fashionable—it was known as Mount Whoredom. During the British occupation it was reported that "whole nights are spent drinking and carousing . . . Here it is confidently affirmed and fully believed there are three hundred females wholly devoid of shame and modesty."

The hill, 60 feet higher than it is now, was covered with huckleberries, brambles, cedars, and cow paths. It was so steep that it was hard to ascend without the help of footholds worn into the surface. This rugged and inhospitable area, originally known as Trimountain because of its three-peaked silhouette, takes its current name from the warning beacon that stood on top of the hill from 1634 to 1789.

!!
Walk straight ahead up Joy Street

You have entered the Historic District of Beacon Hill, but this is not the refined, timeless Beacon Hill of classic photographs and guidebooks. Actually, the hill is divided into three distinct sections: the North Slope, where you are now standing, an area of economic and social transition; the South Slope, consistently upscale, where you will again meet Harry Otis and his friends; and the Flats, a Victorian embellishment built on landfill.

Today, the North Slope is home to an interesting mixture of professionals, students, and artists living in refurbished 19th-century apartment buildings and rooming houses. Emblematic of the demographics, the former police station at **#74 Joy Street [2]** is now Hill House, a community center, nursery school, and home of the Beacon Hill Civic Association. In a creative reuse of space, the cell blocks were converted to a gymnasium. As one Beacon Hill wag wryly observed, "This is a settlement house for the upper middle class."

But as you ascend Joy Street, imagine this neighborhood filled with different dialects and different ethnicities, as waves of immigrants struggled here before moving on. Free blacks established a community in this area years before the Civil War. Their story is the most powerful one.

In 1638, the first slaves arrived in Boston. By the early 18th century, they were an integral part of the hugely profitable "triangle trade" that made fortunes for Boston's early merchant class. Yankee ships crisscrossed the Atlantic, trading in England, Africa, and the West Indies to sell a roster of commodities from fish and silks to rum and slaves . . . nothing was sacred. However, by 1783, when Massachusetts became the first state in the union to outlaw slavery, the city already had a large free black population. Unfortunately "free" did not mean "equal."

Smith Court [3] is the most interesting street on the North Slope and is critically important to Boston's history. The large red-brick building in the middle of the block on your left is the

Turn right onto Smith Court

African Meeting House [4], the oldest African American church still standing in the United States. It was built in 1805–1806 by black laborers and craftsmen, although the funds came from both the black and white communities. Prior to the building of this church, African Americans, both slaves and free, attended white churches in which they were forced to sit upstairs in "Negro pews"; they were never considered full voting members of the congregation. The African Meeting House served as a place of worship but also much more—a school, community center, hideout for runaway slaves, and political rallying base for the abolitionist movement.

January 6, 1832, was a critical night in the history of the African Meeting House—the New England Anti-Slavery Society was created. Its birth, in a small basement schoolroom, was championed by William Lloyd Garrison. Oliver Johnson, Garrison's biographer, wrote:

A fierce northeast storm, combining snow, rain and hail in about equal proportion, was raging, and the streets were full of slush . . . On that dismal night, and in the face of a public opinion fiercer far than the tempest of wind and hail that beat upon the windows . . . was laid the foundation of an organized movement against American slavery that at last became too mighty to be resisted.

This group, dedicated to the emancipation of black slaves, underscored its principles by including women as equal participants and public speakers. In the next three decades, the most famous abolitionist orators appeared here, including the great Frederick Douglass, an escaped slave who became a spokesman for the movement both locally and abroad.

Visit the museum, which encompasses the meeting house and the Abiel Smith School next door. Watch the 15-minute film.

As you leave the museum, note the period colonial houses across the street, residences of prominent blacks through much of the 19th century. Peek up **Holmes Alley [5],** a narrow, dark passage at the end of Smith Court on your left. It was part of the labyrinth of escape routes that foiled slave catchers. For more comprehensive insight into this period of American history, take the 1.6-mile Black Heritage Trail walking tour offered by the National Park Service.

Observe the creeping gentrification as you walk up Joy Street. While the development of the North Slope was a gradual evolution, the development of the South Slope of Beacon Hill was dramatic and brilliantly conceived. No one had envisioned this hilly pastureland as a fashionable neighborhood. But in 1795, the new State House was sited at the crest of Trimountain (see map). Savvy Harrison Gray Otis and his partners hastily formed a consortium known as the Mount Vernon Proprietors. For $18,000, they bought 18.5 acres of land adjacent to the future seat of government from the painter John Singleton Copley, a Tory sympathizer who had fled to England. Gossip had it that Copley felt he had been swindled, for he had no idea that the new State House was being built in his backyard. When he

Walk to back left-hand corner of Smith Court

Exit Smith Court; continue up Joy Street

tried to contest the transaction, he found it to be irreproachably legal, and, in fact, the proprietors, while possibly taking advantage of his absence, paid fair market value.

The first part of the master plan necessitated flattening the top of this craggy peak. An ingenious but simple system was utilized to transport gravel and dirt down the hill, dumping it into the Charles River and tidal marshes and thereby extending the city to what is now Charles Street. "Gravity carts" attached to one another by ropes traveled up and down the mountain on rails. As the heavily laden carts were sent down from the top, the empty carts at the bottom came flying up for new loads. Watching the carts ply up and down the slope was a favorite spectator sport for young boys.

The proprietors conceived a neighborhood of large freestanding houses surrounded by private stables, gardens, and expansive lawns. By 1806, red-brick mansions (many, naturally, designed by Bulfinch) were rising on the old Copley property. As economic times changed, however, the value of the land increased so dramatically, the proprietors could not resist filling in the open spaces with substantial townhouses. These attached homes are much more the norm on the hill today.

Turn right onto Pinckney Street

According to historian John Harris, **Pinckney Street** is the "Cinderella street of Beacon Hill." It delineated the border the Mount Vernon Proprietors arbitrarily created to exclude those who were not of their "society." Its architectural hodgepodge reflects the street's ambiguous position, resulting in an ambience that combines the character of both sides of the hill. Once considered the bohemian street of the hill, it attracted writers, artists, and educators. Today Pinckney Street is particularly attractive to young families because of its proximity to downtown, its manageably sized houses, and its unpretentious charm.

Number 5 [6] on your right, thought by many to be the oldest house on the hill, was completed in 1791, before the Mount Vernon Proprietors had even created Pinckney Street. The plot of land was purchased in 1786 by two free black men. George Middleton was a coachman and a Revolutionary War commander of the all-black company the "Bucks of America." Louis Glapion, his housemate, was a mulatto barber from the French West Indies. Presumably, the bachelors got on well until Glapion married and the house was divided. As you can see, the building is beautifully preserved.

Although most people associate Louisa May Alcott and her family with their home in Concord, Massachusetts, they wintered in at least six different houses on Beacon Hill in the mid-19th century, including **#20 Pinckney Street [7]**. Despite this plethora of homes, they always seemed to be in financial straits. Louisa's father, an educator, was well respected in transcendentalist circles, but concentration on purity and light did not help feed his family. Perhaps the following encomium was his way of thanking the friends who supported them until Louisa became a successful novelist, publishing *Little Women* in 1868: "There is a city in our world upon which the light of the sun of righteousness has risen. It is Boston. The inhabitant of Boston is more pure than that of any other city in America." Somewhat of a burden for contemporary Bostonians . . .

Number 24 [8], whimsically known as "the House of Odd Windows," evolved from a stable to a grocery store to a private home. It is a favorite of architects who laud its original window style, from the eyebrow in the roof to the tinted bull's-eye pane in the front door. Notice that no two windows on the façade are alike.

The dignified structure on the **corner of Pinckney and Anderson Streets** looks more institutional than residential even though it now houses expensive condominiums. This creative rehab is not unusual in Boston, even in historic buildings such as this one. Built in 1824, it was the first home of the English High School, devoted to educating "lads intending to become merchants or mechanics." In the early 1850s, it became the **Phillips School [9],** the first in the city to be racially integrated.

And it is hardly surprising, in this neighborhood where the abolitionist movement began, that **#62 [10]** was once a safe haven for fugitive slaves. Astonishingly, its owner at that time, George Hillard, never acknowledged, and in fact may not even have known, that his wife was helping those seeking freedom. In the 1920s workmen discovered a trapdoor hidden in a closet. Above it was a small, ventilated attic space large enough to harbor several people. Here were found two metal plates and spoons, conceivably used for the last hurriedly eaten meal.

Strolling along Pinckney Street, enjoy the quiet: it is easy to imagine that you are walking on an automobile-free 19th-century town lane rather than in the middle of a bustling city. In spring, the flowering pear trees help recreate an aura of another time, further softening the cityscape. Depending upon the season, the crest of the hill affords a glimpse of the Charles River beyond the city roofs—a favorite vista, especially at sunset.

❗❗
Continue on
Pinckney Street

Peek through the gate of **#74 ½ [11],** mysteriously located between #72 and #74. This entryway, dark and almost medieval, provided privacy for a very public-spirited benefactor of the hill. The secret passageways and private mews of Beacon Hill add authenticity to its 19th-century allure.

Scandale! There are two tales of Beacon Hill murder—one was for money, the other was for love. They were especially titillating because they occurred in "Proper Bostonian" society. In the early 1960s, while living with her grandmother here at **#85 Pinckney Street [12],** 18-year-old Suzanne Clift had a torrid affair with a South American Romeo. She became pregnant, he refused to marry her; she killed him, cut him up, and delivered his privates to his family. Incarcerated in the nearby Charles Street Jail, she was regularly counseled by the nuns of Saint Margaret's convent, which stood across the street from her home in Louisburg Square. Her successful insanity plea delivered her to McLean Psychiatric Hospital in Belmont, Massachusetts, instead of prison. (It is said with a wry and knowing smile that the true Bostonian has a house on Beacon Hill, a pew at Trinity Church, a subscription to the Boston

Symphony, a plot at Mount Auburn Cemetery, and *a relative at McLean.*)

👣
Stop at Louisburg
Square

On your left is one of Boston's most exquisite landmarks. **Louisburg Square [13],** with its classic red-brick bowfront houses, is elegant, restrained, and aristocratic. Graceful in its entirety, the lower side of the square is cited by many authorities as the finest row of townhouses in the United States.

The square was developed from 1834 to 1848 according to a plan initially conceptualized by Bulfinch. It was named after a battle in 1745 successfully fought by the Massachusetts militia against the French fortress of Louisburg in Nova Scotia. Although most Bostonians do not know the derivation of the name, they *do* know that the correct pronunciation is "Lewisburg," plainly American, not "Louieburg," pretentiously French.

👣
Walk around the
square, from lower
to upper side

The 22 original residents created the first homeowners' association in the country, signing an agreement, still in existence, that they would forever maintain their square. Each association member is taxed yearly to maintain the private park. One of the perks of the levy was that when the trees of the park were trimmed, each house received a stack of wood for its fireplaces. Today each house is deeded two parking places on the square, a priceless gift indeed—even more valuable than firewood.

Louisburg Square has been home to many of the rich and famous; the following are a few favorite anedcotes. **Number 20 [14]** saw the 1852 marriage of "The Swedish Nightingale," Jenny Lind, to her long-standing accompanist. The marriage capped her wildly successful 100-concert tour of America. Promoted by the great impresario P. T. Barnum, her concerts were so popular, it was almost impossible to obtain tickets—comparable to rock and pop-music extravaganzas today. At an auction for tickets to the Boston performance, the first ticket brought a bid of $625—a breathtaking amount of money at that time.

In 1934, Louisburg Square was the birthplace of the Boston soirée. Imagine ten genteel couples arriving promptly at 9:00 P.M. at the historic home of Mrs. E. Sohier Welch—the women in their most decorous gowns, the men in full formal attire. Dancing to music on records specially imported from Europe, this was a no-nonsense evening: no smoking or drinking allowed, only the waltz. This abstinence was a testimony to the seriousness of the occasion, as Mr. Welch was a leading wine connoisseur with a collection of Madeiras dating back to the Revolution. These exclusive parties eventually moved on to grander settings and became *the* major charitable events on Boston's social calendar. Seniors today are still nostalgic about the "Boston waltz," with its unique swooping style.

Residents of **#13 through #19 [15]** (on the upper side of the square) were not typical Beacon Hill social doyennes. For over a century these houses served as the convent for the nuns of the Society of Saint Margaret's, an Anglican order. When you return to Pinckney Street, you can clearly see the chapel attached to the back of #19. Known for their good deeds on the hill, the nuns started the library at the Charles Street Jail, having noticed

Houses on
Louisburg Square

the absence thereof when they visited Suzanne
Clift. They were equally well known for the wedding cakes they baked for young brides of the
hill; the proceeds were used to pay off the convent's mortgage. In 1990, feeling there was a paradox between their upscale residence and their
mission, the nuns departed the hill for humbler
Roxbury. The corner house was purchased by
Massachusetts senator John Kerry and his bride,
Teresa Heinz. A complete renovation of the
house and its surroundings was undertaken—
including moving a pesky fire hydrant around
the corner, so the senator would be able to park
in front of his door.

Interestingly, the demographics of Louisburg Square, once considered an aristocratic stronghold, have become much more diverse. Whereas about one third of the houses remain opulent private homes, the majority have been divided into apartments and condominiums. As you leave Louisburg Square behind, note the well-behaved climbing vines. They seem emblematic of the good breeding that has always defined this "proper Bostonian" enclave.

Down Pinckney Street on your left at **#86 [16]** lived civic leader John J. Smith. A member of the Massachusetts House of Representatives, this African American was an early civil rights activist. When he purchased this house in 1878, he was the first black to cross the invisible color line that divided the Boston social landscape.

Turn back onto Pinckney Street; walk downhill one block

You are greeted at **#40 West Cedar Street [17]** by a shop that is both a horticultural and atmospheric gem, Rouvalis Flowers. The changing floral display that often spills out onto the sidewalk reflects the season and ranges from vibrant impatiens to exotic Vanda orchids. Peek inside to glimpse the period tin ceiling and old-fashioned wood-framed refrigerator.

Walking along West Cedar Street, you will actually be backtracking in architectural time. The Mount Vernon Proprietors started to develop the street in 1827. The block you are on, built in the 1830s, is more Greek Revival than Federal, marked by characteristic simplicity and flat-headed entranceways. The next block features earlier dwellings more Federal in character. It is

Turn left onto West Cedar Street

virtually impossible to perfectly categorize many houses on the hill as belonging to only one specific architectural style because the periods do in fact overlap, and many houses include aspects of both. Some were built as hybrids, and others were modified as they were "updated" by new owners.

Because West Cedar traverses the hill, the orientation of the upper and lower sides of the street is different. The gardens of the lower-side houses are accessed through basement doors, whereas the gardens of the upper side are buttressed with raised terraces. These urban gardens are treasured by those living on the hill. The annual garden tour and window box competition are local traditions. To keep the garden tours lively and special each year, the hosts strive for originality. In the mid-1950s, a rather restrained era, a particularly proper gardener, charmed by the exuberance of Neapolitan café gardens, decided she would re-create one in her backyard. For her final note of authenticity she scattered her own freshly washed underwear along clotheslines hung for the occasion. The effect was not what she had hoped for. Visitors were mortified to look upon the undies of their fellow gardener and, eyes averted, swiftly moved on to the next house. The hostess never again opened her garden.

These well-bred ladies, however, were capable of organizing much more than flowers. In 1947, they successfully fought the powerful and popular mayor James Michael Curley (see Downtown and North End Walk) in the "Battle of the Bricks." The mayor wanted to replace the old distinctive brick sidewalks of the hill with cement.

Protesting housewives brought out chairs and baby carriages and camped on their sidewalks all day, refusing to allow work to begin. Curley, an astute politician, realized this was not a battle worth fighting and backed down. No one dared take on the women of West Cedar Street again—and the bricks remain.

Asher Benjamin, Charles Bulfinch's protégé, was responsible for many Federal-style houses and public buildings not designed by his mentor. He lived here at **#9 [18]** in a house of his own design. A later resident at this address was Arthur Shurtleff, a young divinity student. In 1893, he began the tradition of putting lighted Christmas candles in the windows of Beacon Hill houses, a tradition that continues today and gives a 19th-century holiday glow to the neighborhood.

The streets are still gently illuminated with gas lamps as they were in Shurtleff's day. Originally, they were lit every evening by a lamplighter carrying a long pole and were turned off automatically by the city at dawn. In this, our more automated, less poetic era, the lamps burn round the clock, as it is far too labor-intensive to hire a lamplighter.

The enchanting houses of **Acorn Street [19]** were home to members of the service trade fortunate enough to be employed by one of the Great Families on the Hill. These nine buildings, dating from 1828 to 1829, housed a highly privileged class of Beacon Hill coachmen. The cobblestones you see here and scattered around the hill were originally used to provide better footing for horses. Today, they are as valuable as 19th-century antiques. In

Continue walking along West Cedar Street to corner of Acorn Street on left

fact, when the cobbles were removed for utility work in 1991, they were kept in storage and then carefully replaced. Acorn Street residents are fiercely proud of this, the most photographed street in Boston. Whereas the street is intimate in scale, many residents have panoramic views of the city from their hidden roof gardens.

‼️

Continue on West Cedar Street; at end, turn left onto Chestnut Street; walk up left side of street

The last building on your right (corner of Chestnut), with its distinctive iron lyre, is the **Harvard Musical Association [20].** Founded in 1837 by Harvard graduates, its original mission was to expand Boston's provincial musical experience beyond psalms to chamber and symphonic music. In the mid-19th century, the association raised enough money from its sponsors to build a con-

View down
Acorn Street

cert hall to accommodate 2,000 people, rivaling the then-nascent Boston Symphony Orchestra (BSO). Its prominence was such that Richard Wagner approached the association with an offer comparable to his oversized ego. For a mere million dollars cash, he would move to America and allow them to debut his opera *Parsifal*. The issue became moot when Wagner made a deal in Bayreuth. Meanwhile, Henry Lee Higginson, the founder of the BSO, began to sell much less expensive tickets than the association. Although he went into debt (which he could easily afford, see Back Bay Walk), his orchestra put the association's out of business. Smaller concerts continued in different venues until the association was established here in 1892.

To celebrate the centennial at Chestnut Street, a commemorative evening in 1992 replicated the food, decor, and music of its glorious past. Pomegranates, quail, champagne, and oysters presented atop a pair of full-size bucks served as the backdrop for the music popular during the 1890s: Beethoven's *Adelaide* and *Archduke Trio,* two songs by Bach, and Handel's *O, Ruddier Than the Cherry.* Aficionados are welcome to visit their music library, the oldest in the country. It is still a concert venue.

You have just turned onto what many consider the loveliest street in Boston. The simplicity of the architecture is enhanced by the restrained combination of early-19th-century embellishments: wrought-iron railings, brass door knockers, boot scrapers, chimney pots, fanlights, and Greek Revival porticos. Each house thus presents a unique façade, while the street has a pleasing consistency. **Chestnut Street**, developed by the Mount Vernon Proprietors from 1800 to 1830, has changed little since that time. It still exudes an aura of decorum. When high-tech business executives anticipate a transfer to Boston, this is where they imagine living.

The house at **#29A [21]** is thought to be the second Bulfinch house on this site. Built between 1800 and 1802, it has a bowfront addition that architectural historians date circa 1818 because of the use of a different style of brickwork and the presence of pale purple panes of glass. These tinted windows—the result of an accident—became early status symbols. The glass was imported from Germany and was clear when it was installed. When exposed to sunlight, however, its color changed to this lovely hue. Blame (or credit) is due to the inadvertent addition of too much manganese oxide during production. Houses with genuine purple panes can be accurately dated between 1818 and 1825, as it was only during this narrow time frame that this bizarrely behaving glass was manufactured. However, what was once considered flawed became coveted and copied, and, as you walk around the Hill, you can try to determine which panes are the real thing. Cognoscenti can distinguish the authentic panes by the undulating colors in the glass. The word on the street (Chestnut) is that these original panes at #29A are insured by Lloyds of London.

Across the garden, **#27 [22]** is an imposing Gothic limestone edifice built in 1918 as the chapel for Boston University's School of Theology, which was behind it on Mount Vernon Street. In 1965 it was converted to condominiums, complete with underground parking for residents. Although an architectural anomaly, it does not overwhelm the overall harmony of the street.

Matching houses were built for the three Swan sisters at **#17, #15, and #13 [23].** Their mother, the only female member of the Mount Vernon Proprietors, deeded the houses to her daughters, "free and exempt" from the control of their husbands. This was highly unusual, but so was Hepzibah Swan. Colonel James Swan, her husband, amassed his fortune as a privateer (a quasi-legal pirate). While living in France, he convinced the vulnerable aristocracy to safeguard all their furniture and possessions with him until the wave of revolution subsided. Unfortunately for his friends, they lost all their worldly goods as well as their heads. James sent everything to the United States, and Hepzibah furnished homes for herself and her daughters. (Some of this furniture resides today at Boston's Museum of Fine Arts; see Indoor Foot Notes.) Poor James—his reward for being such a good provider was 22 years in a French prison for finagling in the financial markets. And yet, despite her husband's unsavory reputation, Hepzibah was successful in business and society.

Built from 1806 to 1808, these houses are classic Bulfinch: flat façades; stone string courses; graceful, slender entrance columns; and recessed arches around the first-floor windows. Another characteristic is the *piano nobile,* the prominent second floor that contains the formal living spaces. Large windows and wrought-iron balconies draw attention to these important rooms. A whimsical sounding architectural term, "diminishing fenestration," also applies. It simply means the size of the windows decreases from the second floor upward. Classic Hepzibah, determined to prevent sibling rivalry, added her own design element. The stoops of the houses are the same height despite the incline of the hill, as the lower houses have additional steps.

Ironically, the ignominiously acquired Swan furnishings, art, and tapestries served as the setting for meetings of the highly principled Boston Radical Club. Mrs. John T. Sargent, a Swan descendant, hosted these monthly gatherings at #13 from 1867 to 1880. The participating luminaries included poets Henry Wadsworth Longfellow and John Greenleaf Whittier, abolitionists Julia Ward Howe and William Lloyd Garrison, philosophers Henry James Sr. and Ralph Waldo Emerson, and writer Oliver Wendell Holmes Sr. No food was served; the only nourishment was intellectual. As Holmes most modestly observed, "All I claim for Boston is that it is the thinking center of the continent, and therefore of the planet."

Could the erudite Holmes have appreciated the mischief in the following story about him? Walking up Chestnut Street one day, Holmes noticed a little boy stretching to reach the door knocker on a nearby house. Offering his help, Holmes gave the door three good raps. The little boy looked up at his benefactor and exclaimed, "Now run like hell!"

Holmes appears again in a less mischievous, more malevolent tale. He served as a character witness in 19th-century Boston's most notorious murder trial. This one was about money, and it began here at **#8 Walnut Street [24].** George Parkman, a wealthy physician more involved in business than medicine, left his house on the morning of November 23, 1849, and he never returned.

Walk slightly to the right on Walnut Street to #8

He was a snobbish and self-righteous prig who, despite being philanthropic, was also thoroughly dislikable. The last person who saw him alive was Dr. John Webster, a professor at Harvard Medical School. Webster supported his wife and daughters' social aspirations by falling further and further into debt. Parkman was Webster's main creditor, and he hounded him incessantly. Webster acknowledged that he had indeed seen Parkman on the morning of his disappearance, for Parkman had come to collect the $483.64 that he was owed. Webster maintained that he paid the debt and Parkman left.

With a large reward offered for finding Parkman, the whole town got in on the investigation. After four days of searching, including two thorough inspections of the medical school premises, Parkman was not to be found. But the suspicious janitor of Webster's laboratory had a hunch . . . With his wife keeping watch, the janitor started digging into the wall of a dark, dank storage area. And his doubts were confirmed: "The first thing which I saw was the pelvis of a man, and two parts of a leg . . ."

Tickets to the trial were even harder to get than those for a Jenny Lind concert. In order to accommodate all of Boston's voyeurs, a new set of spectators was ushered in every 10 minutes. Never before had one of Boston's First Families

Hidden garden
of Beacon Hill

been involved in a murder. Add to this an unsympathetic victim and a particularly grisly scenario, and you have the stuff of tabloid sensationalism. Although Webster pleaded not guilty, he was condemned to hang. Only in appealing for leniency did he finally confess to the murder and gruesome disposal of the cadaver. Parkman's intolerable taunting had pushed him to strike the fatal blow. But despite strong character witnesses such as Oliver Wendell Holmes, despite the huge wave of public compassion, Webster hanged. Dr. Parkman's mean-spirited behavior was mortifying to his family; they never recovered from the embarrassment of the publicity. The moral of the story: "Neither a borrower nor a lender be."

The house and garden at **#14 Walnut Street [25]** are intriguing. Most Beacon Hill gardens are hidden—this one, elevated just above eye level, is so verdant and alluring, one can't imagine a more privileged urban space. Not only is the garden obscured, but the house's construction is partially under wraps. It is actually built of brick, visible on Walnut Street, but covered in wood on the north and south faces. The wooden overlay was a fairly common Federal technique, but one rarely seen today. Finally, it is known as the "Small House for Little Money." "Things are seldom what they seem . . ."

Turn left on Walnut Street; walk to corner

Affectionately known as Mount Whoredom by the British Redcoats, **Mount Vernon Street** metamorphosed into what Henry James superciliously called "the only respectable street in America." This, the first street developed by the Mount Vernon Proprietors, embodies many of the Federal architectural characteristics associated with Bulfinch: recessed window arches, string courses, and keystone window lintels. The intricate, delicate wrought-iron balconies, fences, and other ornamentation arrived as ballast from Spain and transformed the homes they adorned from stolid to seductive. George Weston, an often-quoted Boston observer, noted, "Black lace is definitely the proper wear for the Federalist type of home."

At end of Walnut Street, cross Mount Vernon Street; turn right and stop at #55

The proprietors themselves are very much in evidence here. One of the original group, Jonathan Mason, built a grand freestanding mansion here in 1801. It no longer exists, but his legacy remains in the two houses he built for his daughters, **#55**

and #57 [26]. Today #55 is open to the public as the Nichols House Museum. Although the bones are pure Bulfinch, the eclectic interior reflects the years during which Miss Rose Nichols was in residence; she died in 1960.

Walk left down
Mount Vernon
Street to end

Numbers 59 through 83 [27] replaced the Mason manse. Here lived one of the famous Cabots who conversed "only with God." One of Boston's wealthy families, the Cabots parlayed family assets into a fortune when scion Godfrey Lowell Cabot realized the potential of the new automobile industry. He had earned a respectable $30,000 a year in 1902 as a producer of carbon black, a pigment used in ink, shoe polish, and paint. Its use in the production of automobile tires catapulted his yearly income to $500,000 by 1925.

The stables for the Swan sisters of Chestnut Street have long since been converted to the charming diminutive dwellings at **#50–#60 Mount Vernon Street [28].** As deeded in 1804, the buildings' height was restricted to 13 feet to permit a view of Mount Vernon Street from the back of the Swan homes. The arched doorway was once functional, not merely decorative; its width allowed access for carriages and cattle.

We meet Harry Otis once again in his magnificent mansion at **#85.** Bulfinch's second house for Otis, built in 1802, a mere six years after the first, reflects both Otis's upward mobility and his marketing savvy: he considered moving to the hill critical to the financial success of the Mount Vernon Proprietors. The sense of expansiveness that one experiences on Mount Vernon Street is a result of a gentleman's agreement between Jonathan Mason and Harrison Gray Otis to set their houses 30 feet back from the street—and this gracious openness has been mandated ever since. This house embodies all the familiar Bulfinch design elements, with the addition of some new detailing such as soaring second-story pilasters, a roof balustrade, and a cupola, which give the house a scale, grace, and grandeur not seen before on the hill.

Despite the elegance of his new home, Otis lived here for less than six years before moving onward and upward. He sold it to a little old lady from Salem for just under $23,000. One 20th-century owner, another elderly lady, lived here alone in one room on the third story, "its floor covered with linoleum and heated by a small free-standing heater." Based on the latest price tag, $12 million in 2003, it seems likely that the house has been upgraded.

The next house, **#87,** was built on land Charles Bulfinch owned. It is said he intended this house to be his own but never lived here: by the time it was completed, he couldn't afford it. For although Bulfinch was the architect everyone hired, no one paid him enough to live in the grand style he created for others. This and its counterpart next door were inhabited by a wealthy banker and a businessman, respectively. If you don't think the houses look purely Bulfinch today, you are right. The left house has been completely rebuilt, and #87 has had a façade-lift.

The massive twin brownstones, **#70–#72,** across the street, are clearly not in the Bulfinch tradition and were built in 1847, later than most houses on this street. The scale of the buildings is testimony to the owners' successful banking careers. Jonathan and Nathaniel Thayer were sons of a rural Massachusetts minister, and their father would likely have been pleased that his sons' homes later became the Boston University School of Theology. Today, the buildings are—you guessed it—luxurious condominiums.

❗❗
Stop at corner of
Charles Street

Charles Street, Beacon Hill's lively commercial thoroughfare, with its range of interesting shops and restaurants, has gone through numerous major transformations. Once under water, it was filled in by the Mount Vernon Proprietors as they leveled Trimountain, solidifying both the land and their investment.

In the 1920s, the street was widened by 10 feet to the contour you now see. Previously, it was prime residential property. At the river end of the street lived the publisher Jamie Fields and his popular young wife, Annie. During the latter part of the 19th century, *le tout monde* attended their entertaining salons. After James's death in 1881, Annie continued the tradition, cohosting with her dearest friend, the author Sarah Orne Jewett. This relationship, in which two independently wealthy professional women lived as a couple, was so well accepted here in literary and artistic circles that it was referred to as a "Boston marriage."

Historian Samuel Eliot Morison, a Beacon Hill resident, reminisced of a picturesque era at the turn of the 19th century, when trolleys emblazoned with bright scarlet, crimson, pale blue, and maroon clanked along

Charles Street with barely a commercial establishment in sight, "not a single antique shop!"

Across the street is Asher Benjamin's **Charles Street Meeting House [29],** originally built in 1807 for the Third Baptist Church. At that time, as the river ran just by the door, it was most convenient for baptisms. It has since been home to three other denominations and a pulpit for social activists from abolitionist Sojourner Truth to antiwar crusader Dr. Benjamin Spock. When the street was widened, the building was taken down brick by brick and reassembled. The façade has been preserved, but like the rest of Charles Street, it too caters to the material, not the ethereal.

Until 1708, Beacon Street was known as Poor House Lane, with the tidal waters of the back bay lapping at the hill. The configuration of Boston is now so different, it is hard to imagine this corner as a malodorous waterfront. As unappealing as this beach scene was, ironically, the fresh spring water discovered here began the evolution of the settlement that became Boston.

Just up the block, near the corner of **Spruce Street [30],** lived the first and only person who could afford a vast tract of land on Beacon Hill. The Reverend William Blaxton arrived from England in 1623 as part of a group that was unsuccessful in settling south of Boston. Rather than return to England, the eccentric reverend migrated north and settled near an excellent water source on what is now the western end of Beacon Hill. Content to live alone, he built a house, planted an orchard, and considered his library of 200 books sufficient company.

Turn left on Charles Street; walk to Beacon Street; turn left and walk to State House at top of hill

He enjoyed his solitude for five years until the arrival of the Puritans of the Massachusetts Bay Company. Their settlement in nearby Charlestown was failing because their water was contaminated. Blaxton generously offered to share his fresh supply. What a mistake! In 1630, the Puritans moved in, lock, stock, and Bible, and could not resist proselytizing. Blaxton, an Anglican, managed to live with his neighbors for two years before selling them his land for £30 sterling and fleeing to Rhode Island's more tolerant clime. Fifty acres of this land were set aside for common use, and they remain so today, as the Boston Common across the street. It was, in fact, America's first public park.

Blaxton returned only once, to find himself a wife. He then hurried back home to what is now the Blackstone Valley (Blaxton, Americanized) of Rhode Island.

Walking up the hill, you may feel transported to London of the 1850s. Charles Dickens noted with pleasure how much the street reminded him of home. Oliver Wendell Holmes imperiously dubbed this street "the sunny street that holds the sifted few." From Blaxton's uninhabited refuge, to Poor House Lane, to the *crème de la crème* in 220 years . . . One hundred and fifty years later, it looks and feels quite the same as Holmes described it. He christened the patrician class who lived here as Brahmins, a "harmless, inoffensive, untitled aristocracy," with "their houses by Bulfinch, their monopoly on Beacon St., their ancestral portraits and Chinese porcelains, humanitarianism, Unitarian faith in the march of the mind, Yankee shrewdness, and New England exclusiveness"—a pithy characterization of one's own clique.

"An elegant new house" was how Harry Otis's third home at **#45 Beacon Street** was recorded by Boston town assessors when he moved here in 1806. By now you will recognize all the Bulfinch Federal touches that characterize the façade. As on Mount Vernon Street, the house was free-standing, with a stable yard on the downhill side and a capacious English garden on the uphill side. Inside it was equally grand, with 11 bedrooms and 12 fireplaces serving the needs of Harry and his wife Sally, seven children, and a half dozen servants. And they lived the lavish life. Harry, the flamboyant social tycoon, placed a 10-gallon Lowestoft bowl filled with punch (spiked, of course) on the stair landing every day: it encouraged his guests to take refreshment on their way up to the drawing room, where he held court. It is said that Harry, despite 40 years of gout, breakfasted daily on *pâté de foie gras.* He thrived here for 42 years, dying at the age of 83. When he married, he set a life goal of amassing an estate of $10,000, quite respectable in those days; he died a man of considerable influence and wealth, with his annual income greater than his lifetime dream.

The lifestyle of the rich and famous in the first half of the 19th century was rather extravagant; nevertheless, some aspects of domestic life were still quite basic. There was no plumbing. All water came from an outside well. Privies for this house were located in an ell accessed through the woodshed in the back courtyard. They were pumped out weekly by horse-drawn tank wagons, nicknamed "the Brighton Artillery," for the noise they made as they labored along the cobblestone driveways and streets. Another type of uproar was generated by H. L. Mencken's 1926 satirical treatise stating that, in 1845, bathtubs were "banned in Boston" as health hazards. For well into the 20th century, Mencken's hoax was accepted as fact. That Otis's grandchildren were marched weekly to a public bathhouse for a good tub scrubbing could be true or all wet.

The house was acquired by the American Meteorological Society in 1951 from a single woman who had no immediate heirs. A gentleman friend, a member of the society, persuaded her to bequeath her home to this nonprofit organization with a caveat to maintain the integrity of the original building—and so it has. Despite the drab office furniture now occupying Bulfinch's lovely spaces, it is easy to envision the house in its glory.

What happened to the spacious garden? A sacrifice for the children. In 1831, Otis gave up half his garden to build an attached brick home for his daughter. His wife, Sally, however, would not give up the shape of the bow window in her dining room, so it now juts out into the wall of **#44,** the house next door—overlooking nothing. The rest of the garden was sacrificed in a real estate deal. Otis sold it to his neighbor David Sears, who built **#43** as an addition to his adjacent mansion.

The massive granite edifice, **#42,** is actually more imposing now than when it was built. This, the first true Greek Revival home on the hill, was

View of Beacon Hill
doorway

purchased by the exclusive Somerset Club in
1872. The third floor as well as the barrierlike
front wall were added shortly thereafter. By the
1890s, club life was integral to a Boston gentleman's daily routine. He would stop in after work
for a drink and a game of cards and often return
after dinner if his wife was not as entertaining as
his fellow members. Typically this gentleman's
wealth was at least three generations old; he was
Episcopalian, or possibly Unitarian; most certainly he went to Harvard and spent his days at a
bank or a law firm. According to Brahmin descendant Crosby Forbes, "If you had a Copley
painting that was a good thing; Gilbert Stuart
was not quite good enough." It is ironic that 100

years after the Revolution, there was more cachet in owning a painting by a Tory sympathizer than an American patriot.

The rarified aura of the club lasted well into the 20th century. Boston's famous Irish mayor James Michael Curley, defiantly proud not to be accepted here, would victoriously march up Beacon Street on election night, giving a less-than-polite raspberry to the sour faces looking down from the Somerset windows.

Today, the club membership is more diverse—even women are allowed. To keep this and other Boston clubs solvent, the membership roster includes those with humbler beginnings. According to *The Boston Globe*, young Brahmins are more apt to devote their lives to Internet start-ups, social enterprise, and family, rather than club life.

The lovely twin houses at **#40 and #39** were built in 1819 by one of Bulfinch's protégés, Alexander Parris. The lavender windows prominent against the white interior shutters are originals. The owners made their money in commerce and were lifelong friends. Nathan Appleton, who lived at #39, became the father-in-law of Henry Wadsworth Longfellow. The poet's marriage here to his beloved Fanny was the social event of the 1843 season. After the wedding party, the bride and groom drove by moonlight to their very own mansion in Cambridge—a wedding gift from Fanny's father (see Cambridge Walk).

Number 33 [31] was the home to which the Parkman family fled after their patriarch's notorious murder. They lived here from 1853 to 1908, their desire for seclusion respected by Boston society. When George Francis Parkman, the last surviving family member, died, he left the house to the City of Boston and bequeathed $5.5 million for maintenance of the Common. Today the house is used by the mayor for official entertaining.

Finally—the *raison d'être* for Beacon Hill, the **State House [32]**. The cornerstone was laid on July 4, 1795, by Governor Samuel Adams and Grand Master of the Grand Lodge of Masons, Paul Revere. Fifteen white horses transported the stone to the site in a ribbon-bedecked carriage. The horses represented the 13 original states plus the two newest, Kentucky and Vermont. Judges, farmers, Native American chiefs, and city folk alike participated in the patriotic revelry, celebrating the nineteenth anniversary of America and the promise of the Commonwealth's future.

Walk to front entrance of the State House

Designed by Bulfinch, the building was completed in 1798 at a cost of $133,333.33, five times the original estimate. It has undergone many changes since then. It began as a dignified symmetrical building of red brick with white trim. The wings that have been added east, west, and north have increased the size of the building tenfold. Historian Walter Muir Whitehill amusingly described today's State House as "a very odd fowl indeed—with a golden topknot, a red breast, white wings and [in the back] a yellow tail."

The dome too has undergone numerous transformations: originally it was a shingled cupola; in 1802 Paul Revere and Company covered it with copper sheathing; from 1861 to 1872 it was gilded with 23-carat gold leaf; during World War II it was painted gray to camouflage it from potential air attack; and in 1969 it was regilded. The pine cone at the top has been a constant; a symbolic tribute to the importance of the lumber industry of New England. It is possible here to imagine the original height of Trimountain—it stood as tall as the top of today's State House.

Though Whitehill thought of the building as a fowl, there is something fishy going on inside. Another tribute to the Massachusetts economy is the carved-pine Sacred Cod that has adorned the House of Representatives since 1789. It was held in such reverence that when mischievous Harvard students stole it in 1933, all business in the House ceased. The Harvard "fishermen" finally gave up their catch after several days, so the business of state could resume.

A tale that is neither fish nor fowl but amphibian concerns Republican governor Elbridge Gerry. In 1812, realizing that his party needed more votes, he reconfigured congressional districts north of Boston. When a local engraver published a drawing depicting the new districts, it distinctly resembled a salamander. A reader observed that it looked more like a "gerrymander" to him—hence, the term for questionable redistricting.

Statues of Massachusetts notables flank the perimeter of the site. Interesting but conflicting stories abound about **Major General "Fighting Joe" Hooker [33],** who commands his steed to your right. His name is familiar, but not because he was particularly successful as a Civil War leader. Rather, his name is associated with the women whom he allowed to accompany his troops. They became known as "Hooker's Women," and many people think this is the derivation of *hookers*, a term for prostitutes. However, the term predates the general. It was in usage before 1845 and probably derived from a New York City red-light district known as "The Hook."

The **Shaw Memorial [34]** is a powerful, poignant depiction of a moment in Civil War history. It commemorates the Massachusetts 54th Regiment. Led by 26-year-old Boston Brahmin Robert Gould Shaw, it was the first free black troop to fight for the Union. On May 28, 1863, they marched through cheering crowds in Boston on their way to battle. This regiment would prove that black soldiers were as capable as whites and deserved opportunity for promotion and equal pay. The great abolitionist Frederick Douglass counted two of his sons among these soldiers.

In their courageous attack on Fort Wagner in South Carolina, outnumbered two to one, Shaw and many of his men were killed—a mere two months after their glorious send-off. Intending disrespect, the Confederates buried Shaw and his soldiers together in a mass grave. Rather than view this action as an insult, Shaw's abolitionist family considered it an honor and persuaded the Union army to leave their son buried with his men.

In 1883, the prominent sculptor Augustus Saint-Gaudens was commissioned to portray the regiment departing Boston. Although it may now

!!
Cross street to Shaw Memorial directly opposite State House

seem patronizing to show the white commander on his horse, elevated above his troops, the frieze was considered remarkably progressive at the time because most of the tableau depicts and honors black soldiers. Equally unusual in its time was Saint-Gaudens's use of black models, so he could realistically portray a variety of faces. It took him 13 years to complete this profoundly moving work.

!!
Walk down steps
to view back of
monument

The dedication in 1897 was attended by one of the survivors, Sergeant William Carney, the first black man to receive the Congressional Medal of Honor. It was bestowed upon him for bravery and for recovering the regiment's flag, despite four bullet wounds. Sadly, at that time, only the names of the white officers were engraved on the back of the monument. It was not until 1984 that the names of the 62 brave black soldiers were added. The movie *Glory* was based on this event.

Ideas and ideals have always been integral to the fabric of **the Common [35].** Historically a multi-use facility, it accommodated preachers, poets, and lovers as well as hangings, pillories, sheep, and cattle. It was also a campground for the redcoats. The gallows, the livestock, and the British soldiers are gone, but the Common is still the place for politicking, picnicking, and promenading.

One imagines that these paths have been privy to many intimate conversations. A particularly charming anecdote from *Literary Trail of Greater Boston* involves the usually eloquent Oliver Wendell Holmes, who recounted his own bumbling marriage proposal, made while strolling along the

Common's Long Path. Unable to speak directly, he found his metaphor in the environment by asking the future Mrs. H., "Will you take the long path with me?" "Certainly," she replied, "with much pleasure." "Think," he said, "before you answer: if you take the long path with me now, I shall interpret it that we are to part no more," and so it was.

And here our "long path" comes to an end.

The **Park Street T Station [36]** was the terminus for the first subway in America, which opened on September 1, 1897. The mosaic mural by the turnstile depicts the first streetcar as it entered the tunnel; a female passenger brandishes that historic day's *Boston Globe*. This new underground transit system was viewed as the solution to Boston's traffic problems—although the first line was only six-tenths of a mile long. Reformer Sylvester Baxter was ecstatic, if not far-sighted, in his assessment of the first subway: "The completed subway is a marvel of convenience and public comfort with its enameled walls, its brilliant electric illumination, its sweet and wholesome air, its commodious stations where people await their cars sheltered from wind and rain, from summer heat and winter cold—everything as cleanly as the traditional Dutch housewives' kitchen." Bostonians were so excited to ride on the new system that on the first day more than 100,000 passengers paid five cents to make the trip. By the end of the first year, more than 50 million passengers had taken that same ride.

Walking back down to Charles Street on the Common side of Beacon Street will allow you to

‼

Addendum choice #1: If you intend to leave Beacon Hill, walk through the Common parallel to Park Street to Park Street T station appreciate the stateliness of "Poor House Lane." The corner of Beacon and Charles is well known to all fans of Robert McCloskey's children's book *Make Way for Ducklings,* for it was here that Officer Clancy and colleagues stopped traffic so that Mrs. Mallard and her eight ducklings could cross the street to rejoin Papa in the Public Garden (see Back Bay Walk).

Addendum choice #2: If you wish to spend more time on Beacon Hill, walk down Common side of Beacon Street; meander along Charles Street; explore the Flats

If you are inclined to eat or shop, you may have found the perfect location. Known for antique stores, Charles Street also boasts a range of other shopping and eating opportunities. And if you are still enchanted by Beacon Hill, the captivating streets west of Charles, known as the Flats, are warrens of atmosphere and architectural fascination. Of particular interest are the refurbished stables and coach houses on lower Chestnut Street, once known as Horse Chestnut Street; the Victorian Church of the Advent at Mount Vernon and Brimmer Streets; and the faux 17th-century West Hill Place and Charles River Square, which were actually built in 1910 to replicate London architecture.

Harrison Gray Otis and Charles Bulfinch would have been pleased that the property values they anticipated have soared beyond imagination. Yet they certainly never envisioned that the Beacon Hill they created would extend beyond Charles Street into what was then the water of the back bay. It is a credit to Bulfinch's architectural genius that so much of Beacon Hill remains as he designed it. Leaving Beacon Hill for other neighborhoods, we wryly recall his naive observation that there would be no need to train his children as architects, for there would be nothing left for them to build.

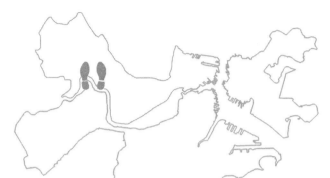

Cambridge

"You can always tell a Harvard man . . ."
—James Barnes, 1866–1936

Essential Information for Walk Three

Length of walk:	scant 2 ¾ miles
Terrain:	flat
Time:	2 ½ hours at a leisurely pace, without museums or detours listed below
Nearest T stop:	Harvard Square on Red Line
Starting point:	Exit T at main escalator; walk to back of escalator enclosure and walk right, crossing Dunster Street; stop in front of Au Bon Pain, facing yellow building across Massachusetts Avenue

Supplements to the Walk

Highly Recommended

Ware Glass Flowers at Harvard Botanical Museum
Time:	35 minutes
Hours:	daily, 9:00 A.M.–5:00 P.M.
Telephone:	617-495-3045
Admission:	$9; discount for seniors, students, and children; Sun. free
When:	second third of walk, at 26 Oxford Street

Mount Auburn Cemetery
Time:	1–2 hours
Hours:	Oct.–Apr.: daily, 8:00 A.M.–5:00 P.M.; May–Aug.: daily, 8:00 A.M.–7:00 P.M.
Telephone:	617-547-7105
Admission:	free
When:	end of walk; take #71 bus from Mt. Auburn Street post office (15-minute bus ride); most spectacular in spring and fall

Of Further Interest

Arthur M. Sackler Museum
Time:	1 hour
Hours:	Mon.–Sat., 10:00 A.M.–5:00 P.M., and Sun., 1:00–5:00 P.M.
Telephone:	617-495-9400
Admission:	$9; discount for seniors, students; and children free; Sat. A.M. free
When:	first third of walk at 485 Broadway

Harvard Museums of Cultural and Natural History
Time:	1–2 hours
Hours:	daily, 9:00 A.M.–5:00 P.M.
Telephone:	617-495-3045

Admission: $9; discount for seniors, students, and children
When: second third of walk at 26 Oxford Street

Guided tour of Longfellow National Historic Site
Time: 45 minutes
Hours: summer: Wed.–Sun., 10:30 and 11:30 A.M. and 1:00, 2:00, 3:00, and 4:00 P.M.; call for hours during other months
Telephone: 617-876-4491
Admission: $3; children free
When: second third of walk at 105 Brattle Street

Detour through West Cambridge neighborhood
Time: 45 minutes
When: second third of walk

Browse and lunch in Harvard Square
When: end of walk

Massachusetts Institute of Technology (MIT)
Time: 1–2 hours
Hours: daily, 9:00 A.M.–5:00 P.M., on your own; or student-guided tours, Mon.–Fri., 11:00 A.M. and 3:00 P.M.
Telephone: 617-253-4795
Admission: free
When: end of walk; take #1 bus from Holyoke Center in Harvard Square to 77 Mass. Ave., Building 7 (Rogers Building); 15-minute bus ride

Cambridge - Walk Three

1. Holyoke Center—Harvard Yard
2. Wadsworth House
3. Massachusetts Hall
4. Harvard Hall
5. Hollis Hall
6. Statue of John Harvard—University Hall
7. Widener Library
8. Memorial Church
9. Sever Hall
10. Emerson Hall
11. Carpenter Center
12. Fogg/Busch-Reisinger Museum
13. Sackler Museum
14. Gund Hall
15. Memorial Hall
16. William James Hall
17. Adolphus Busch Hall
18. University Museums of Cultural and Natural History
19. Tanner Fountain—Science Center
20. Austin Hall
21. Christ Church
22. Gutman Library
23. Stoughton House and Vassal House
24. Episcopal Divinity School
25. Longfellow National Historic Site
26. Society of St. John the Evangelist
27. Newell Boathouse
28. Weld Boathouse
29. Larz Anderson Bridge
30. Weeks Bridge
31. Peabody Terrace
32. Harvard Lampoon Building
33. Apthorp House
34. U. S. Post Office

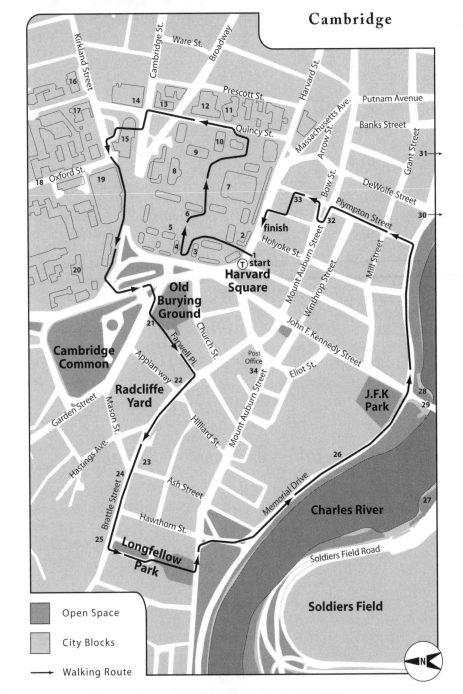

Cambridge

Kirkland Street
Cambridge St.
Ware St.
Broadway
Prescott St.
Cambridge Street
Quincy St.
Harvard St.
Massachusetts Ave.
Arrow St.
Putnam Avenue
Banks Street
Grant Street

16
14
13
12
11
17
15
31
9
10
18 Oxford St.
19
8
7
Bow St.
DeWolfe Street
30
33
6
5
32
Plympton Street
4
2
20
3
finish
Mount Auburn Street
Winthrop Street
Mill Street

1
start
Harvard Square
Holyoke St.

Old Burying Ground

21

Farwell Pl.
Church St.
John F. Kennedy Street

Cambridge Common

Appian way
22
Post Office
34
Eliot St.

J.F.K Park
28
29

Radcliffe Yard

Garden Street
Mason St.
Hilliard St.
Mount Auburn Street
26

Hastings Ave.
23
Ash Street
Memorial Drive
27

Brattle Street
24
Hawthorn St.
Charles River

25
Longfellow Park
Soldiers Field Road

Soldiers Field

	Open Space
	City Blocks
→	Walking Route

N

The most opinionated zip code in America
—The Boston Globe, 1991

‼

Stand on terrace in front of Holyoke Center (Harvard Information Building) **[1]** between Dunster and Holyoke Streets, facing mustard-colored building across Massachusetts Avenue

To paraphrase Mark Twain, in New York, they care about your net worth; in Philadelphia, it's your pedigree; in Boston, it's your academic credentials. The pervasive influence of Harvard University sets the tone.

Today's parade of avant-garde youth leavened with professorial tweed and spiced with street people selling newspapers and causes hardly reflects the demeanor of the Puritan forebears who founded the village of Newtowne here in 1630. The Puritans' life was rigidly circumscribed by their religious beliefs, yet they held education in such high esteem that one of their first communal acts was to establish a "colleg" in 1636. The Massachusetts Great and General Court allocated £400 sterling—one quarter of its annual taxes—to fund the colonies' first university. Two years later the settlement was renamed Cambridge, honoring the English institution where many of the Puritans had been schooled. The academic environment has nourished intellectuals, writers, and educators ever since. And it was here that the mandate for professors to "publish or perish" began with America's first university press.

The new university was named after its benefactor, John Harvard, a Charlestown minister who died shortly after his arrival from England (see Waterfront and Charlestown Walk). He bequeathed all of his library and half of his

£1,700 estate to the "colleg." His generosity was due in part to his friendship with Nathaniel Eaton, Harvard's first president. Luckily for the institution, Harvard died before learning of his old friend's Dickensian behavior. Eaton was summarily fired after it became known that he flogged the school's nine students with a "cudgel big enough to have killed a horse." Furthermore, his wife's cruel gruel included "mackerel with guts in them and goat's dung in their hasty pudding."

To appreciate the real value of John Harvard's donation, in 1655 tuition was £2. If students did not have this amount in currency, they could pay with a combination of cash and barter—firewood, food, rum, or furs. The rigorous curriculum included Greek, ethics, Hebrew, ancient history, logic, and grammar. Latin was not taught because fluency in the language was a prerequisite for entry. It is often assumed, incorrectly, that the purpose of the college was to educate ministers, probably because so many of the early graduates became clergymen.

The tenor of the school changed dramatically in the subsequent 30 years. By the 1680s the atmosphere in Cambridge had become much more liberal than that of conservative Boston (not unlike today). The college's fifth president, the Reverend Increase Mather, came to "radical" Harvard after preaching belief in the premise but not the excesses of the Salem witch trials. However, upon his dismissal in 1701, he censured the school as "Godless Harvard," condemning its "lack of religious stamina."

Across Massachusetts Avenue—known nearly universally as Mass. Ave.—stands **Wadsworth House [2],** a mustard-colored clapboard building on the site of Master Eaton's first college hall. Eaton's cruelty was replaced by institutionalized gentility. Built in 1726, this structure housed Harvard's presidents until 1849. Early Georgian in style, its leitmotif is distinguished by symmetry, a hipped roof, prominent dormers, and a triangular pediment over the front door. It was most impressive in its heyday, with its large gardens, stable, and coach house. According to Harvard historian Samuel Eliot Morison, it hosted "ladies in the drawing room, a band in the back parlor, governor and aides and other distinguished foreigners, arriving and departing . . . ice cream and coffee circulating all the time." More significantly, Wadsworth House was where George Washington created his successful strategy to liberate Boston from the British occupation.

👣

Cross Mass. Ave.; enter campus on left side of Wadsworth House; stay on main path to center of the Old Yard

In Washington's day, the campus area you are entering was called "college yard" to differentiate it from the abutting cow yards. Prior to the tenure of President Kirkland in 1810, this well-kept area, with its stately old elms and crisscrossing pathways, was "an unkempt sheep-commons" replete with privies and brew houses.

As you stroll into what is now known as the **Old Yard,** the enthusiastic energy of today's students invites one to contemplate the spectrum of youth who have passed through these gates over the past 370 years. Harvard is the alma mater of seven American presidents, the first of whom was John Adams, class of 1755. His was a strenuous routine, punctuated by the college bell and defined by study and prayer. The 5:00 A.M. tolling announced the beginning of each predictable day: 6:00 A.M. prayers, breakfast of beer and bread, classes that lasted well into the afternoon, a respite of intramural ball or cricket, more classes, 6:00 P.M. dinner, required study, and at last, the 9:00 P.M. curfew.

A hundred years later Harvard life had become more frivolous. The experience of upper-class historian Francis Parkman was typical of his generation. His regimen was defined by parties, social clubs, hunting along the Charles River, and rowing at nearby Fresh Pond. He found this routine so depleting that he had to take a year off to do the European grand tour.

Well into the 19th century, Harvard's hierarchy was based on social class rather than achievement. Each freshman was ranked by the college president according to his parents' position in society, and this placement determined everything, from when he was served at the dinner table and recited in class, to where he was seated in chapel and his rank as he marched in processions. The stereotype of the Harvard man—"You can always tell a Harvard man, but you can't tell him much"—began to change after World War II. University Professor Helen Vendler recalls the Harvard of her youth: "When I first saw the Yard in the forties, I was touched by the uniform handsomeness of the young men stepping quickly across the Yard in their wool jackets and silk ties. Now the young come in both sexes, and wear many costumes—and the sight is more amusing and more democratically reassuring, if not so beautiful."

Today 20,000 students are enrolled at Harvard; 6,700 are undergraduates. This diverse group represents every state and more than 100 countries. Students can choose from more than 1,000 courses, including Greek and Hebrew, although study of these languages is no longer required.

👣

Stop at Massachusetts Hall, the red-brick building at left before the main gate

What *is* required is that freshmen live in or near the Old Yard, and it is rumored that only the quietest, whose taste runs to classical music, live in the upper stories of **Massachusetts Hall [3]**. On the lower floors are offices of the president, the provost, and other high-ranking administrators. One noteworthy resident is the ghost of Holbrook Smith, purportedly of the class of 1914. He visits students at the start of each semester and seems perfectly normal, although no one has ever seen him enter or exit. Smith is thought to be the rightful owner of any liquor that mysteriously finds its way into the rooms of underage students. A long-term proctor who "met" him once acknowledged that this would be an appropriate abode for an amiable apparition, stating, "Eighteenth-century buildings should have ghosts. If there are going to be ghosts, it makes sense that they should live in the nicest building in the Yard." This building is, in fact, the oldest on campus and was built as a dormitory in 1720.

👣

Walk to main gate

The little **guardhouse** just inside the main gate has generated remarkable controversy, considering its size. It was completed in 1983 at an amazing cost of $57,000 because local architect Graham Gund had to submit over 300 drawings before the Cambridge Historical Commission would approve the design. It's not only Harvard men whom you can't tell much.

This is the third incarnation of **Harvard Hall [4]** on this site. The first rotted after 30 years, and the second, completed in 1677, was totally destroyed by a 1764 fire. At the time it was a multi-use building, "compleat" with classrooms, chapel, laboratory, and the largest library in the colonies. The book collection numbered over 5,200 volumes and included John Harvard's original bequest. The fire was a disaster—only one book of the collection survived. As the devastated President Holyoke surveyed the ashes, he was approached by a young student, eager to save the day. He sheepishly admitted having removed a book, *Christian Warfare Against the Devil, World, and Flesh* to finish studying in his room that night. Although he had broken a rule, he knew Holyoke would be grateful that at least one of John Harvard's books remained to begin the rebuilding of the library. Holyoke was indeed grateful, thanked the young man, and then summarily expelled him for taking the book without permission. So much for diligently completing your homework.

Harvard Hall was rebuilt and a fire engine purchased. **Hollis Hall [5]** residents formed an "Engine Society" and used their new vehicle more for fun than for putting out fires. Professors who gave too much homework were often "mistakenly" hosed down, as were fellow stu-

Walk to next red-brick building, Harvard Hall, across from Massachusetts Hall

Return to main path; walk left to next building, Hollis Hall

dents sitting in temptingly open windows. The old college pump, which stood across from Hollis, provided all the water for this frivolity as well as for more practical needs. But it too fell victim to a collegiate escapade and was blown up in 1901. The one you see now is a 1936 replica.

Note the concave pavement in front of Hollis Hall—damage incurred from disposable "radiators." The cold yet ingenious students who resided here shortly after the Revolution appropriated unused cannonballs they found in the Yard, heated them in dorm fireplaces, and carried them upstairs to warm their drafty quarters. Each spring a barrage of cold cannonballs rained from the upper-floor windows.

Hollis has evoked remarkably different reactions from its famous residents. Architect Charles Bulfinch (see Beacon Hill Walk) so admired it that he built neighboring Stoughton Hall as its twin. Author Henry Adams was so miserable here that he described it as "the coldest, dirtiest and gloomiest [dormitory] in Cambridge."

‼
Walk across the
Old Yard to statue
in front of gray
granite building,
University Hall

Interestingly, John Harvard never registered a personal reaction to the place, as he was never here. Yet according to Nobel laureate poet Seamus Heaney, "A spirit moves, John Harvard walks the yard," and this spirit is embodied in Daniel Chester French's bronze of 1884, affectionately nicknamed **"The Statue of Three Lies" [6]**. First, this is not John Harvard's likeness—French used a contemporary Harvard student as a model, since no one really knew what John Harvard looked like. Second, Harvard was not the founder, just the first benefactor. And third, the college was founded in 1636, not 1638. The nice irony is that the statue's base also bears the college crest, which boasts the motto *Veritas*, the Latin word for truth.

The austere and imposing **University Hall [6]** standing behind the statue is Charles Bulfinch's most well-known contribution to Harvard. This edifice, housing administrative offices, looks dignified, yet it was the setting of notorious food fights in the 19th century. Bulfinch had designed four separate dining rooms, one for each class, separated by walls but united by a large round opening in each wall. These openings, an architectural feature intended to create harmony between the spaces, instead facilitated disharmony in the form of flying food and hurled epithets.

Conceived in 1813 as the core of the growing campus, University Hall looks very much now as it did then, but the campus has far outgrown Bulfinch's vision. In comparison to the colonial intimacy of the Old Yard, the **New Yard** projects an aura of grandeur. In 1936, the space was gloriously transformed into what is still known as "Tercentenary Theater" to commemorate the 300th anniversary of Harvard's founding. The ceremony was carried on despite pouring rain, and as one sardonic attendee observed, "This is [President] Conant's way of soaking the rich." Now, this "theater" is where first-year students are welcomed and graduates are bid farewell.

Walk around right side of University Hall into the New Yard

The two most prominent buildings of the New Yard are **Widener Library [7]** on your right and

Memorial Church [8] on your left. Some observers feel the juxtaposition of these two dramatically different structures is awkward. But Chiang Lee, an eminent artist and observer of the 1950s, is more poetic in his assessment.

> *Being no student of architecture I found the clean white spire of the University Chapel facing the splendid façade of the Widener Memorial Library, with its Corinthian columns and broad flight of granite steps, an unusually pleasant balance of elegance and grandeur. One might expect a long stretch of wide open ground in front of the Widener Library to enhance its majestic bearings, but the trees in the Yard suggest depth instead. Without the trees, the University Chapel might look too exposed and too genteel in comparison with the strong colonnade of mighty stone pillars of the Widener Library. As it is, the two buildings exchange smiles over the treetops and through the holes between the leaves.*

Inside Widener 3.5 million volumes are stacked on over 50 miles of shelves. This, the largest academic library in the United States, was built in 1914 to honor Harry Elkins Widener, a Harvard graduate who went down with the *Titanic*. A bibliophile, he was returning from a book-buying trip in England. An unconfirmed story alleges that Harry was about to step into a lifeboat when he ran back to collect one of his newly acquired prizes; he never made it back on deck. His mother, who was rescued, wanted to memorialize her son and put an ad in a Philadelphia newspaper soliciting ideas. Harvard had one. Mrs. Widener donated Harry's books and $2 million for the construction of a library. She chose the architect and design and further stipulated that the exterior of the building could not be changed. Two additional requirements were a bit more eccentric: (1) every Harvard student had to pass a swimming test in order to graduate because she believed her son might not have drowned had he known how to swim; and (2) ice cream, Harry's favorite food, had to be served in every dining hall at every meal. The former has been suspended since the 1970s because of its bias against physically disabled students; and the latter is, to the best of our knowledge, changed only by the addition of frozen yogurt. Daily, students and faculty ascend the long staircase up to Widener's front doors; unfortunately, the facility is closed to the public.

Memorial Church was built in 1931 to honor Harvard's war dead from World War I. Its Georgian style belies its 20th-century origin. This nondenominational Protestant house of worship is very much a part of the community—its morning service regularly starts the day for a loyal constituency, and its Sunday service is broadcast on Harvard radio. The design is unusual—it appears that two porticoed entrances exist, but one can only enter on the side facing the Old Yard. The strong Doric columns on the south face successfully balance massive Widener Library. Its steeple, modeled after Christ Church in Boston's North End (see Downtown and North End Walk), is a revered Harvard landmark.

Sever Hall [9] is H. H. Richardson's (see Back Bay Walk) brilliant contribution to the New

Continue to far side of New Yard, stopping at Sever Hall, to right of Memorial Church

Yard. Its mysterious aura is defined by its elaborate but somber design. Romanesque in style, it is characterized by turreted towers and a powerful entrance arch. The romance of the arch is enhanced by its "whispering gallery"—if you speak quietly into one corner, a companion in the diagonally opposite corner should be able to hear your message. The variety of window openings is an integral part of this design and, with the lively brickwork, makes the building engaging rather than forbidding.

Robert Campbell, architectural critic for the *Boston Globe* suggests "that people should go and watch Sever. Watch it change. The delicacy of detail is something you're not going to pick up the first time around . . . Best of all are the decorative panels that are set into the walls . . . The work is intricate, and you have to watch a panel for a while before the imagery begins to come clear. It's heavy on animals and flowers." Campbell challenges his readers to find the pair of elephants carved into one of Sever's façades. "If you can do that, you can say this is a building you've thoroughly watched." Although built in 1880, Sever's style is simpatico with its 18th-century neighbors in the Old Yard.

‼
Stop at Emerson Hall, to right of Sever Hall

Not often are students and professors so simpatico. But according to one story, poet Gertrude Stein, then a Radcliffe student, must have been surprised when the great philosopher, Professor William James, treated an apparent act of rebellion as a sign of wisdom. Beginning her final exam here in **Emerson Hall [10]**, Stein wrote in her blue book, "I don't want to take this exam, it's too nice out," and walked out into the spring air. James's response was unexpected: he returned her test book, noting, "Miss Stein, you truly understand the meaning of philosophy, *A.*"

How should the viewer truly understand the meaning of the Henry Moore sculpture *Four Piece Reclining Figure,* on your left as you leave the Yard? Its elegant simplicity and sensuous curves pull you in and tantalizingly defy you to see the figure as a single entity. According to Jeremy Knowles, who was a long-time dean of the faculty of arts and sciences, the best way to understand the statue as a unified piece is to stand outside the gate and view the work from between the 37th and 38th bars as you walk to your left.

Leave the New Yard via stairs to left of Widener Library

The contour of the Moore sculpture is a perfect segue to the only work in North America by the French architect Le Corbusier—Harvard's **Carpenter Center for the Visual Arts [11].** According to the *AIA Guide to Boston,* it is "a piece of sculpture designed for human use." Depending on where you stand the building may seem curvilinear or angular in form. Its thin vertical pillars make it appear to float above ground level: it is difficult to imagine how the building is really supported. When Le Corbusier came for the dedication in 1963, he is said to have had a similar reaction, feigning surprise and exclaiming to the contractor, "My gosh, man, you've built it upside down." Walk up the ramp to see the open studios and display spaces that define the purpose of the building—to encourage participation in the visual arts.

Continue in same direction on Quincy Street

❗❗

Stop at corner of
Quincy Street and
Broadway

The traditional exterior of the adjacent **Fogg/
Busch-Reisinger Museum [12]** gives no hint of
its Italianate interior. The courtyard of travertine
marble is modeled after a church in Montepul-
ciano. Unfortunately, the museum is being reno-
vated and will not re-open until 2013. However
the **Sackler Museum [13]** across the street, a
repository of ancient, Asian, Islamic, and Indian
art is graciously sharing its space. Harvard Art
Museum docent Alice DeLana advises that "the
Sackler Museum . . . has been completely rehung
to include highlights from the Fogg and the
Busch-Reisinger as well as wonderful new paintings and sculptures and works from storage that
have not been seen for decades . . . The underlying philosophy of the new installation is 'aesthetic
resonance,' which roughly means that objects and
images have been placed in unexpected proximity
to each other—modern next to old, demure next
to assertive, shocking abstraction next to photo-
graphic realism."

The Sackler exterior is also notable but controversial. When it was unveiled in 1985, it was
widely criticized as inharmonious with the
other buildings on the Harvard campus.
Stunned, the Sackler's English architect, James
Stirling, countered, "Doesn't fit in? What do
you mean 'it doesn't fit in'? I've simply created
another animal for Harvard's architectural zoo."
As you look around at the disparate building
styles—the Carpenter Center, the Fogg, Gund
Hall behind the Sackler, Memorial Hall's tower
rising on the left, and the white rectangular
Henry James Hall in the distance—the variety
of architectural styles poses an interesting ques-

tion. Should an institution construct new buildings that are complementary to existing structures, or should it generate excitement and architectural exploration as it continues to grow?

Gund Hall [14], housing the Graduate School of Design, has been touted as a brilliant example of form following function. Aspiring designers and architects work in a huge, open, multilevel space flooded with natural light. Their communal studio encourages the sharing of ideas. The stairway silhouette is most dramatic at night, when you

Cross Broadway and walk to Cambridge Street; stop opposite stepped concrete building

Memorial Hall

can see the students hunched over their drafting boards into the wee hours.

👣

Cross Cambridge and Quincy Streets to near side of Memorial Hall

One wonders if any of today's design students are inspired by the extravagant **Memorial Hall [15].** Designed by two Harvard alumni, Henry Van Brunt and William Robert Ware, it was erected to honor Harvard men who died while fighting for the Union during the Civil War. It evokes a strong reaction, usually favorable, though it has had its detractors. This commanding Ruskinian Gothic edifice (see Back Bay Walk) has been part of Harvard since 1878, and writers have alluded to it ever since. Here it is described by a southern gentleman in Henry James's novel *The Bostonians:* "The ornate, overtopping structure . . . was the finest piece of architecture he had ever seen . . . He thought there was rather too much brick about it, but it was buttressed, cloistered, turreted, dedicated, superscribed, as he had never seen anything; though it didn't look old, it looked significant; it covered a large area, and it sprang majestically into the winter air."

Jane Langton's 1978 mystery, *The Memorial Hall Murder,* provides a less favorable assessment: "The building rose above him like a cliff face, mess piled upon mess, ten thousand of brick laid upon ten thousand. It was ugly, majestically ugly. Augustly, monumentally ugly."

👣

Walk inside through main central doors

Regardless of how you feel about it, it is impossible to ignore this resplendent giant, with its cathedral-style windows and multicolored slate roof. And walking into the splendid transept, with its stained-glass windows, Gothic vaulting, and 28 white marble panels, is awe inspiring. The panels are engraved with the names of 136 Harvard men and the Civil War battlefields on which they died. Interestingly, the 64 Harvard men who died fighting for the South are not consecrated here. The freshman dining room, Annenberg Hall, on your left, is off limits to nonstudents. Sanders Theater, on your right, is open only when lectures or concerts are scheduled. But not all is reverential here. Local folksinger Cheryl Wheeler has likened singing in the wood-paneled Sanders Hall to performing inside an enormous rolltop desk.

Leave Memorial Hall through doors on far side of transept

As you leave Memorial Hall, you might imagine yourself in the company of the regular subscribers to Boston Symphony concerts held here for the Harvard community in the 1920s. And how quintessentially Harvard they were, according to Marian Cannon Schlesinger's memoir:

Cambridge ladies were, however, even frumpier than their Boston counterparts and though often "dressed" for these occasions gave the impression of being garbed out of their grandmothers' trunks. These being evening concerts, one was at least spared the ill-favored hats worn by generations of Boston ladies, which in their Cambridge incarnation might have been even more disastrous. Not that anyone really cared or noticed. Their minds were on higher things.

Stand outside Memorial Hall, with Kirkland Street in front of you

Many strolled home to Professors' Row a few blocks away, where houses were known by who had lived in them rather than actual street addresses. In those days it was rare for a nonacademic to penetrate this intellectually exclusive enclave. Today, if you wish to explore this professorial neighborhood, walk to your right to Francis Avenue and Irving Street, which are just beyond **William James Hall [16],** Harvard's first skyscraper. This 1965 tower must have shocked its traditional neighbors and still dismays many. But Harvard is always needing more space and at some point had to expand upward.

What a contrast between the severe James Hall and the whimsical **Adolphus Busch Hall [17]** next to it! Architectural critic Douglas Shand-Tucci appraises Busch Hall this way: "One feels overwhelmingly the sense of having stumbled into some railroad station on the Orient Express." Its exuberance reflects the profession of its benefactors, beer magnate Adolphus Busch and his son-in-law, Hugo Reisinger. Built in 1917 to house Harvard's significant Germanic art collection, it was not opened until 1924 because of the strong anti-German sentiment generated by World War I. Today the collection can be found at the Fogg, and Busch Hall houses the Gunzberg Center for European Studies.

And behold, next door, a chirpy **yellow and white residence** built in 1838. It has had many incarnations and was once actually located down the street; but the one constant has been its cheerful demeanor. It is presently the home of the Reverend Peter J. Gomes, Preacher to the University and Plummer Professor of Christian Morals. Despite his ponderous title, Reverend Gomes is known for his accessible style and commitment to community.

Walk left on
Kirkland Street
to the end

Glass flower from
the Ware Collection

A remarkable community resource well worth a detour is located down Oxford Street, to your right. The **University Museums of Cultural and Natural History [18]** are actually four museums, all housing superb exhibitions, and one that is absolutely unique. If you have time to visit just one, we highly recommend the **Botanical Museum's Ware Glass Flower Collection.** Father and son Leopold and Rudoph Blaschka worked on this project from 1887 to 1936, creating more than 3,000 models (of more than 830 plant species) known for their beauty and botanical accuracy.

The Blaschka technique—shaping the softened glass by hand—has never been duplicated.

Another combined effort of man and nature, **Tanner Fountain [19],** is on display in front of the Science Center. The circular rock formation conjures up the harsh New England countryside and is softened by the miracle of water—a cooling spray in summer and misty steam in winter. Man has enhanced the landscape by turning lights on at night and turning the fountain off on windy days.

The **Science Center [19],** one of the busiest buildings on the campus, was completed in 1972 under the direction of José Luis Sert, former dean of the School of Design and prolific Cambridge architect. In order not to overshadow the historic buildings of the Old Yard across the street, Sert chose to combine boxy components to create a functional whole. So unusual in its design and lack of symmetry, it became the subject of a long-held myth that its precast concrete sections were held together by epoxy. By grafting—not gluing—three new glass boxes onto the original building, contemporary architects Andrea Leers and Jane Weinzapfel have honored the functionality of Sert's original design.

The architectural amalgam of Harvard's multiple campuses reasserts itself as we leave the 20th-century Science Center and approach Harvard Law School. Established in 1817, it is the oldest existing law school in the country. You may recognize the distinct Romanesque style of H. H. Richardson in **Austin Hall [20].** His concern for color, unique brickwork, and

👣 Walk straight ahead to the Science Center

👣 Continue to walk straight ahead, keeping Science Center and large granite Littauer Hall on your right; look right to Austin Hall

arched entryways mark this building as well as Sever Hall. He playfully included his initials within the decorative carving . . . yours for the finding. It is interesting to note how perceptions change: this building, once considered garish, now seems so harmonious.

Cross Mass. Ave. to Cambridge Common

The green park ahead of you is the **Cambridge Common,** established in 1631. It originally consisted of 86 acres, set aside and fenced in to safeguard cattle from predatory wolves and hostile native raiders. Commercial interests reduced the site to its current 16 acres. Where you now see young men and women playing baseball, more than two centuries ago you would have seen young men readying for war. We entered the Harvard campus at the site of George Washington's first local headquarters, and we leave where he first took command of his troops. July 3, 1775, was George Washington's first official day at work, two weeks after the Battle of Bunker Hill (see Waterfront and Charlestown Walk). Gathered on the Common were more than 20,000 New England militiamen, increasing the population of Cambridge more than tenfold. Although the numbers were great, Washington's opinion of his men was not:

I found a mixed multitude of people here, under very little discipline, order, or government . . . I have already broke one Colonel and five Captains for cowardice and for drawing more pay and provisions than they had men in their companies . . . In short they are by no means such troops, in any respect, as you are led to believe of them from the accounts which are published, but I need not make myself enemies among them by this declaration, although it is consistent with truth. [There is] an unaccountable kind of stupidity in the lower class of these people which, believe me prevails but too generally among the officers of the Massachusetts part of the Army who are nearly of the same kidney with the Privates, and adds not a little to my difficulties.

Walk left on sidewalk, parallel to Mass. Ave.; cross Garden Street to island

The **William Dawes Memorial Park** commemorates "the other rider," a gentleman most certainly worthy of Washington's respect. To ensure that the minutemen of Lexington and Concord knew that the redcoats had started their advance ("one if by land, and two if by sea"—see Downtown and North End Walk), the Boston patriots sent out two riders on the fateful night of April 18, 1775, heralding the beginning of the Revolutionary War. As Paul Revere rowed across the Charles River from downtown Boston and then rode on horseback from Charlestown, Dawes took the longer land route through Cambridge. Longfellow's poem "Paul Revere's Ride"—"Listen, my children, and you shall hear / Of the midnight ride of Paul Revere"—scanned well but left out Dawes. His ride is immortalized here in brass hoofprints imbedded in the pavement. Despite Washington's misgivings about the competence of his men, the Cambridge minutemen, rallied by Dawes, fought bravely at the Battles of Lexington and Concord; many lost their lives and are buried in the cemetery across the street from this memorial.

Cross to far side of Garden Street; stop at cemetery

The **Old Burying Ground** dates back to 1635. It is the egalitarian final resting place for many of

Cambridge's early settlers—ministers, Harvard presidents, slaves, and patriots. The melancholy array of gravestones contributed their part to the Revolutionary War effort. Many of the markers once bore metal identity plates, which were melted down to make ammunition. Douglas Shand-Tucci muses that it is "best to see this burying ground on a wintry mid-day of bare tree limbs and slate sky, snow in the air, pale sun fading. Who was it who said—surely a Puritan, and surely of New England—fall is best, winter truest?"

Shand-Tucci's evocation of a winter sky also eloquently expresses the spare beauty of colonial architect Peter Harrison's (see Downtown and North End Walk) **Christ Church [21]** of 1759. Its original Anglican parishioners were Tory aristocrats who departed on the eve of the Revolution. The church was abandoned until December 1775, when, at the suggestion of his wife, Martha, George Washington had it spruced up for New Year's Eve services. Martha looked spiffy, dressed in a peach-colored satin dress, accompanied by George and by fife and drums. Alas, it was but one night of glory. This lovely building suffered desecration and pillage during the war because it represented the English privileged class. Here too the patriots scrounged for metal to make bullets, pilfering the organ pipes and window sashes. The church was not fully refurbished until 1825. Sit inside for a few moments to enjoy its understated beauty; even the dazzling crystal chandeliers dating from 1935 harmonize with the austere interior.

Continue right on Garden Street to Christ Church

‼️

Take path at left of
church, emerging
on Farwell Place;
continue to end of
Farwell Place; look
across street

The same restraint continues on picturesque **Farwell Place.** It is a surprise to find this quiet 19th-century enclave one block from the cacophony of Mass. Ave. While some of the homes are still private, others have been recycled into academic offices. Another reincarnation is the former home of Dexter Pratt, celebrated in Longfellow's poem "The Village Blacksmith"; it currently houses the Hi-Rise Bakery and the Cambridge Center for Adult Education. The "spreading chestnut tree" lost in the widening of Brattle Street has been immortalized not only by the poem but also by the wrought-iron replica on the wall across the courtyard from the **Blacksmith House.**

‼️

Walk right along
Brattle Street

Gutman Library [22], on your right, and most of its neighbors house Harvard's Graduate School of Education. The library's expansive windows allow the outsider to see what is going on inside; the unusual below-ground exposure and set-back landscaping make the building less overpowering. These architectural elements create the impression of an "open classroom," a feature of educational theory very much in vogue when the library was built in 1972.

‼️

Note Radcliffe Yard
on right, between
Appian Way and
Mason Street

One hundred years earlier, Harvard's classrooms were hardly "open." Arthur Gilman, an illustrious Cantabrigian seeking higher education for his daughter, envisioned a place where university professors would teach young women the same subjects they taught their male students. Although he had low expectations for the "experiment," Harvard's President Eliot approved Gilman's proposal, and the redoubtable matrons of Cambridge took over, using their considerable influence to establish a "Society for the Collegiate Instruction of Women" in 1879. Fifteen years later it was incorporated as Radcliffe College, named after Harvard's first female donor. Classes were strictly single sex until 1943, when all classes in Harvard's Faculty of Arts and Sciences were opened to Radcliffe students. President Conant quipped, "Harvard is not coeducational in any respect except in point of fact." Twenty-two years later, this same observation was echoed by Faye Levine, the first female executive editor of *The Harvard Crimson:* "Being at Radcliffe means nothing more than being a girl at Harvard. It is a tricky business since everyone knows there are no girls at Harvard." Today the institutions are completely merged, with Radcliffe serving as an institute for advanced study.

Brattle Street, also known as Tory Row, was named after Thomas Brattle, an early treasurer of Harvard. In his day, the mile-long street contained just seven pre-Revolutionary mansions and their extensive gardens. The population was as homogeneous as their homes. Their taste was lavish, their politics English, their religion that of the Crown, their social network closed and exclusive. After the Revolution, when these Tories had returned to England, the composition of the street changed both architecturally and socially. Today, a walk on Brattle Street is a course in American domestic architecture, from the original 18th-century colonial mansions to 19th-century Greek Revival and Victoriana, from early 20th-century Edwardian to contemporary design.

Across the street is the 1883 **Stoughton House [23],** a shingle-style mansion visible behind a

Stop at far side of Mason Street

high brick wall. This truly American architectural vision is noted for its harmonious combination of free forms and repetitive shingle sheathing that wraps around the entire building. Its aura is akin to the somber Sever and Austin Halls on Harvard's campus. It is in fact a younger sibling, designed by H. H. Richardson.

!!
Continue a few
steps until you are
across from gray
house with black
shutters

The **Vassal House [23]** has had an intriguing history. One of the original Brattle Street mansions, it was home to bon vivant and gambler Henry Vassal. High living led to an early death. His widow, Penelope, squared his debts before leaving for the West Indies. Despite being a Tory, she was respected for her integrity and was allowed to take all her possessions, save her medicine cabinet. The house was converted to a military hospital headed by a well-known and respected patriot, Dr. Benjamin Church. His integrity was also unassailable, but his true loyalty was to the British. His duplicity was conveyed to General George Washington by Church's "lady friend," who turned out to be more a friend to the Revolution than to her lover. In 1775 the nascent nation did not yet have laws against treason; Church was shipped out, and he died at sea.

The **Episcopal Divinity School [24]** on your right, part of a consortium of theology schools, stands in marked contrast to the improprieties of Vassal House. Its most famous dean, Bishop William Lawrence, was a model of 19th-century decorum and modesty. He would allow public commemoration only after his death "In remembrance of God's Great Goodness," which he defined as "wife and seven children—and not one of these has ever caused me an hour's pain by any misconduct." The campus feels quintessentially Victorian with its pudding stone, stained glass, and spiritual ambience.

Perhaps Brattle Street's most illustrious resident was the 19th-century poet and scholar **Henry Wadsworth Longfellow.** For generations most American schoolchildren have known him as the author of the poems "Paul Revere's Ride" and "The Song of Hiawatha," but few of us realize his poetry introduced familiar phrases such as "the patter of little feet," "ships that pass in the night," and "into each life some rain must fall."

Continue along Brattle Street to Longfellow National Historic Site [25]

In 1837 he arrived in Cambridge from Maine, a young Harvard professor who spoke 8 languages and read 12. Needing a place to live, he made inquiries that led him to the gracious home of the widow Mrs. Andrew Craigie, who was letting rooms to support her beautiful home. She mistook the clean-shaven and youthful Longfellow for a student and almost refused him a place until he convinced her that he was, in fact, faculty. He fell in love with the house and was particularly enamored of the rooms that served as George Washington's second Cambridge headquarters during the early months of the Revolutionary War. Six years later, he fell in love again, this time with the wealthy Fanny Appleton. Her father bought the house as a wedding gift for the young couple.

They soon became the toast of this very literary town. Their prominent circle of friends included Hawthorne, Emerson, Holmes, and Dickens. But tragedy struck in 1861: Fanny died when her skirt caught fire. Henry rushed to help, yet was unable to save her. He too was terribly burned, and shortly thereafter he grew the familiar beard to hide his disfigurement. He stayed in their cherished home, raised their children, and died 21 years later. The Longfellow family kept the house until 1971, when it became a National Historic Site [25].

It looks very much as it did when it was built in 1759 as one of the original Tory residences. The Craigies had added a few embellishments that did not dramatically change the house's glorious High Georgian exterior. The mansion takes the Wadsworth House architectural vocabulary and makes it both grander and more formal with pilasters, a larger front entrance, and exterior molding. This building has become such a Cambridge landmark that the color is appropriately named Longfellow Yellow on paint charts. The interior, filled with the memorabilia of Fanny and Henry's extensive European travels, reflects their Victorian sensibilities.

Teacher, translator, and America's unofficial poet laureate, Longfellow's popularity was due, in part, to his accessibility. Because he was committed to making his work available to all classes of society, he published simultaneously in both hardcover (leather) and paperback (pamphlet). Longfellow's sales would be considered extraordinary even today. *The Courtship of Miles Standish and Other Poems* sold 25,000 copies in the first two months. Even more astonishing, it sold

10,000 copies in London on the day it was released. In a familiar cycle, Longfellow was deemed obsolete by subsequent generations of writers. Yet he still had many admirers—an especially noteworthy one was poet and fellow Cantabrigian Robert Frost, who used a Longfellow line to title his first book, *A Boy's Will*.

And at this point you must decide whether to pursue "the road not taken . . ."

Meandering around the neighborhood is a favorite pastime of locals. If you have time, this mile-long detour offers a glimpse of upscale Cambridge living, and you can adjust the length of the walk. We suggest the following route: continue on Brattle (many of the houses have historical markers); turn right onto Reidesel; turn left onto Brewster (look for the marker on the Robert Frost residence); turn right onto Appleton; turn right onto Highland; turn right onto Sparks; at Brattle turn left to return to the Longfellow House.

Follow route described in this paragraph, or cross Brattle Street to park

This rectangular green, leading down to the Charles River, was once part of the Longfellow estate, and, in fact, you are walking the path that the poet took down to the river to bathe. Today a memorial stands where the tidal marsh flooded when the river was high. The bust of Longfellow (a copy of Daniel Chester French's original) is surrounded by a bas-relief of six of his literary heroes. The Longfellow heirs gave the land to the public to preserve their father's favorite vista, and today it is enjoyed by residents, both two- and four-legged.

Walk through park to Mount Auburn Street

‼

Turn left onto
Mount Auburn
Street; at corner of
Hawthorn Street,
cross both Mount
Auburn and
Hawthorn Streets;
continue on
Hawthorn, bearing
left, around curve
to Memorial Drive

Also appreciated by man and dog are the paths along the **Charles River.** Both Cambridge and Boston take pleasure from their shared waterway—for most of the year boaters, joggers, bikers, roller-bladers, and children in strollers add action and color to this mixed-use facility. The river's original Indian name, Quineboquin, is onomatopoeic: it means "twisting" or "circular." The 60-mile route that the river travels from Hopkinton to Boston, starting and ending points shared by the Boston Marathon, is more than twice the length of the runners' course. Take time to revel in the beauty of the river.

Not only is the river seductive, but the sycamores flanking it are also extraordinary. They nearly became victims of urban development until the government was intimidated by a force of formidable Cambridge women. In 1963 they chained themselves to the trees and triumphed in their "Save the Sycamores" campaign.

‼

Stop at church on
your left

The wall that fronts the Episcopal monastery of the **Society of Saint John the Evangelist [26]** provides its residents with a contemplative, private space amidst the hubbub of urban traffic. The chapel, however, is open to visitors throughout the day. Subdued on the outside, the interior is a small jewel of early Gothic design.

‼

Continue on
sidewalk along Memorial Drive; stop
just past
middle of park,
then walk to corner

This park was the original site chosen by the Kennedy family for JFK's Memorial Library. They thought the location was particularly appropriate, as the president had hoped to have his papers archived at Harvard, his alma mater. He even thought of teaching at the university after his term in office. But after a decade of planning and fund-raising, the family's intentions were dashed by community opposition to a monumental edifice and the fear of congestion caused by hordes of visitors. The library is now dramatically sited overlooking the water on the southern tip of Boston (see Indoor Foot Notes), and this green has been dedicated to the memory of President Kennedy.

The three athletic facilities within your view represent two opposing visions of sports at the beginning of the 20th century. **Newell Boathouse [27]** across the river and **Weld Boathouse [28]** diagonally across the street stand as testimony to Harvard's oldest and most genteel competitive sport. Both structures were built in the early 20th century: the popularity of rowing was by then well established. A winning anecdote tells how Harvard got its moniker after a race in 1858. Future Harvard president Charles W. Eliot, racing in a six-man boat, bought crimson handkerchiefs for his crew to wear so that the crowd, and especially his fiancée, could identify them. They crossed the finish line in record time, and Harvard athletes have been sporting the crimson ever since.

Architect Charles McKim designed the **Harvard Stadium** across the river with less gentlemanly activities in mind—it is reminiscent of a Roman amphitheater. You can just make out the classical arches of its upper level against the sky, beyond and above the Newell Boathouse. The structure was completed in 1903 for the relatively new game of football. Yet many were opposed to Harvard men engaging in this ferocious competition;

the most vocal was President Eliot, the aristocratic rower. The matter was of such import that President Teddy Roosevelt (an alum) gathered the coaches of Harvard, Yale, and Princeton, along with President Eliot, at the White House. This high-powered huddle resulted in new rules that made the game less brutal, and they were adopted by the collegiate athletic association. President Eliot lost yardage—and football has been played here ever since.

Ever since 1662, when a wooden drawbridge, the Great Bridge, stood here, this has been the site of a major river crossing between Cambridge and Boston. In fact, William Dawes galloped across it on his way to alert the minutemen. Today's bridge, the **Larz Anderson [29],** built in 1912, is far more artistic, and so is the story attached to it. Until recently, a tiny plaque embedded in the brickwork commemorated the tragic life of Quentin Compson, who committed suicide by jumping into the Charles on June 2, 1910. *The Boston Globe*'s Marcella Bombardieri observed, "What the plaque really marks, then, is a geographical point where real and fictitious Boston converge," for Compson was a Harvard student who lived only in the pages of William Faulkner's novel *The Sound and the Fury*. No one really knows who put up—or removed—the two-by-four-inch epitaph, "Quentin Compson. Drowned in the odor of honeysuckle. 1891–1910"—an evocative tribute to the power of Faulkner's words.

Nine hundred real and very determined first-year students land each September on "Baker Beach" at the **Harvard Business School,** where they have little time for water sports, or Faulkner. The expansive grass "beach" rolls out to the river from the grand Baker Library, named after philanthropist and financial wizard George F. Baker. In 1924, he donated the full $5 million needed to build the fledgling graduate school. He was asked to give only $1 million to start the funding campaign but wanted the privilege of building the whole institution: he strongly believed that a rigorous business education would lead to higher ethical standards. Radcliffe women of the 1940s reminisce about how they would sneak across the river to date B-School boys, as their intellectually snobbish friends considered these swains mere tradesmen. Today, approximately one third of the student body are women.

There has always been a rivalry between Harvard and Yale, and this was ironically demonstrated by a philanthropic gesture by Edward S. Harkness, a Yale graduate. He too was eager to donate a substantial amount of money to a university, in this case, his alma mater. His offer to create a residential college system at Yale was rejected. Huffily, he turned to Harvard, the *other* ivy, and thus **Harvard's House System** was born here along the Charles. In 1930 President Lowell eagerly accepted $13.2 million to build Harvard's first seven houses. Subsequently, six more have been added. After freshman year, students are randomly assigned to a house, which differs from a dormitory in that each offers its own dining room, library, tutorials, small classes, and extracurricular activities. Although each house has its own personality (just ask any

Cross street at light; stroll along Memorial Drive, taking in Harvard Business School across the river and undergraduate houses on your left

Harvard grad), they stand along the river as a cohesive red-brick representation of erudition, refinement, and tradition.

Practicality was the *raison d'être* for the **Weeks Bridge [30]** spanning the river in front of you. Romance is the by-product. Its original purpose was to conceal the pipes carrying steam to the new buildings across the river. Built in 1926, it

Weeks Bridge

was named after a distinguished Massachusetts politician in the hope that this tribute would diminish local resistance to a new university incursion. Today another kind of steam is generated by the sensuous dancers of the Boston Tango Club, who perform here by the light of the full moon from spring through early fall. A truly transporting experience! The view of the bridge is lovely at any time, but especially so when the sun is low and the river shimmers with color.

Peabody Terrace [31], the tall multifaceted buildings rising downriver behind the Weeks Bridge, is a residential complex designed by José Luis Sert. When built in 1964, its inventive design, with a playful yet functional façade, was considered an exciting addition to the landscape, providing much-needed housing for young graduate school families . . . affordable, with no frills. According to critic Robert Campbell, "like many late modernists, Sert loved exposed concrete as an honest and muscular material that you could mold into any shape. He liked to set splashes of bright color against its textured gray—'like a parade of elephants and parrots,' in his words."

It has stood the test of time, particularly in comparison to the new graduate dormitory built in 2003, directly across the river. This controversial behemoth in the skyline, now much maligned, may one day be considered a favorite animal in the Harvard architectural zoo.

You are now enveloped by the egalitarian Harvard House System, but as we approach Mount

Make first left onto
Plympton Street;
walk to Mount
Auburn Street

Auburn Street, we move back in time: another era and lifestyle are represented by the Victorian lodgings and elite final clubs in the surrounding neighborhood. Before the house system existed, most students lived in crowded conditions, with plumbing in the basement and no central heating. Developers realized an opportunity to "accommodate" wealthy students and built upscale apartment houses in this enclave, known as the **"The Gold Coast."** The former domain of Harvard's upper crust looks less than luxurious today, but Claverly, Randolph, and Westmorely Halls had amenities ranging from swimming pools to squash courts to elevators. As reported in *Collier's Weekly* in 1912, "Each dormitory had its uniformed servants on watch at the door—butlers ready to receive a card on a tray or ready to run the minor annoying errands."

FDR was one of the privileged few who lived here between 1900 and 1904. His suite is being re-created to reflect the aura and the era of his undergraduate years. The master of Adams House, a Roosevelt relative, is eagerly taking the lead in this $250,000 restoration. The fundraising festivities in 2009 started off with a dinner comparable to one served to FDR's freshman class: oysters and beef Richelieu. Visiting Roosevelt scholars will not eat as richly, but they will live as richly when housed here while doing their research.

The final clubs, somewhat comparable to fraternities at other schools, represented a scant 15 percent of the student body, and their membership reflected the exclusivity of Boston society. The Porcellian was the premier club, yet its façade on Mass. Ave. is the epitome of ordinariness. To those in the know, this was the *ne plus ultra* of inner sanctums. Cleveland Amory, in his book *The Proper Bostonians*, tells of Porcellian member Grenville Clark's bad form. He was already an established New York lawyer (once a Porcellian, always a Porcellian) and brought a guest to the club—New York governor Al Smith—who, having heard so much about the place, prevailed on his patrician friend to give him a tour. Later, during World War II, Clark brought round a second guest, General Dwight D. Eisenhower, whereupon he was harshly reprimanded. Members pointed out that he had brought in more guests than any other Porcellian in history.

On the other hand, ***Harvard Lampoon*** members don't take themselves quite so seriously. Their building **[32]** seems to smile: the round windows are its eyes, the glass lantern its nose, and the front door its mouth, open in an expression of astonishment. Topped off with its copper hat, it is a man bemused and amused. This is the home of the oldest humor magazine in America and has served as the springboard for many writers, from Robert Benchley to John Updike. Frivolity has always emanated from this cheerful building; "Poonies" are known not only for literary flights of fancy but also for their escapades. One of the most notorious Poonie pranks was stealing the cherished Sacred Cod from the State House (see Beacon Hill Walk)—bringing the business of state to a standstill until it was returned.

At corner of Mount Auburn Street, cross street; walk left to front of oddly shaped building on island

The ultimate Poonie prankster was young William Randolph Hearst, who would go on to create the Hearst publishing empire. His business acumen saved the Lampoon from laughing its way into bankruptcy in the early 20th century, and this building is a result of his largesse. Alas, his generosity to his instructors ended his Harvard career: he presented each of them with a mischievously painted chamber pot inscribed with the recipient's name on the inside.

👣

Walk around the far side of the Lampoon; cross Bow Street; continue walking up Plympton Street; walk through gate on your left halfway up block; walk into courtyard to front of large yellow house. (This gate is occasionally locked; if so, continue to corner and turn left onto Mass. Ave.)

Apthorp House [33], one of Cambridge's oldest and most elegant homes, is also a building that made a statement—this time by British loyalists. The house, completed in 1761 for Anglican minister East Apthorp, was so elaborate and luxurious that it was disparagingly referred to by the neighboring Congregationalists as "the Bishop's Palace." Young Apthorp (only 28 when he moved in here), minister at Christ Church across the square, was in the forefront of the Tory flight to England, leaving in 1764. During the Revolution, the American troops quartered here especially appreciated the wine cellar he abandoned.

Once freestanding amid six acres of land that extended all the way down to the river, Apthorp House is now completely enclosed by Victorian Gold Coast buildings. Today the master of Adams House resides here. Claverly, Westmorely, and Randolph Halls are owned by Harvard and inhabited by Adams House students. Butlers are a thing of the past—and the pool is used for theatrical productions.

You now return to the theatrics of everyday life that is **Harvard Square,** where the diversity of age, clothing, ethnicity, and language reflects Cambridge's heterogeneity. The interaction of rushing students, daring skateboarders, window-shopping tourists, strolling dog-walkers, and itinerant street performers creates a dynamism that is both visual and visceral. Joining this throng along

👣 Walk out through gate on far side of courtyard; turn right onto Linden Street; at corner, walk left on Mass. Ave.

Harvard Square

Mass. Ave. you will pass #1304, with its Art Nouveau façade bequeathed to the Museum of Fine Arts; Leavitt & Pearce Tobacconists, with its tin ceiling and early-20th-century memorabilia; and the unprepossessing frontage of the Porcellian Club at #1324.

Take a break at José Luis Sert's imposing **Holyoke Center [1],** home to the Harvard Information Center, where we began our tour. Here you can get a snack or lunch, pick up a *Harvard Gazette* to see what's doing in town, or just sit out front and watch the world go by. If you are a chess player, you might want to challenge the Master for a $2 fee. This Harvard dropout has been stationed here since 1982 and rarely loses. When interviewed by the *Gazette,* he ruminated, "What do I like about chess? You can't win a political argument, but chess—there's an argument you can settle!" But if it doesn't get settled, you can consult the renowned Cambridge law firm Dewey, Cheatam & Howe. As you explore the square, you will find it upstairs from Curious George.

!!

Addendum
choice #1:
Cross street at
Holyoke Center;
board #1 bus to MIT

For those even more curious . . .
Whereas the walk you have just taken covers the heart of historic Cambridge, there is much to visit both east and west, easily accessible by the buses that stop across the street. Cambridge's other great university, **Massachusetts Institute of Technology,** lies 15 minutes east, just beyond Central Square. This vibrant area, very different from Harvard Square, is becoming more gentrified—at an alarming rate, to some observers. But the emphasis here is still

on ethnic restaurants, funky merchandise, and futon shops.

Just beyond this eclectic neighborhood is the architecturally sedate MIT. Its low gray buildings have been likened to a "robust lichen colony." Yet there are some dramatic architectural standouts, including two buildings designed by Eero Saarinen. His cylindrical, windowless nonsectarian chapel is an exquisite spiritual space that shuts out external stimulation. Kresge Auditorium is just the opposite— huge and open—a great tent that seems to float above ground level. Most notable is Frank Gehry's brilliant and controversial Ray and Maria Stata Center, housing computer, information, and intelligence sciences. This crazy-angled, loose-limbed building practically gyrates before your eyes. In comparison to its boxlike, flat-footed neighbors, it seems to dance down the street. Yet, despite being a hallmark of high technology, the Stata Center leaks!

As befits an institution of science, MIT buildings are most often referred to by their numbers, not their names, and you may start your tour at Building 7, the main administration building on Mass. Ave., where you can pick up self-guided tour pamphlets or join one of the two daily student-led tours. Sailors and model boat aficionados should not miss the Hart Nautical Museum in the basement.

Few realize that it was here at MIT that the esoteric scientific measurement, the smoot, was discovered. In order to measure the length of the

Mass. Ave. Bridge (officially named the Harvard Bridge), Oliver Smoot's fraternity brothers flipped him over, head-to-toe, from Cambridge to Boston. The bridge measured 364 smoots plus one ear. Although the bridge has been refurbished since this amazing discovery of 1958, its smoot markers remain. It is public knowledge that a smoot equals 67 inches, but the length of Smoot's ear is an MIT secret.

!!

Addendum choice #2: Consult map for location of U.S. Post Office **[34]** on Mount Auburn Street; board #71 or #73 bus to Mount Auburn Cemetery

For those more interested in the soul than the mind, **Mount Auburn Cemetery** is a 15-minute bus ride west. A tribute to the dead and a sanctuary for the living, America's first garden cemetery, opened in 1831, covers 170 rolling acres, with more than 4,000 trees, 130 species of shrubs, and 30,000 annuals. More than 80 species of migratory birds drop by on their way north. For bird and plant enthusiasts it is a required stop; for many local birdwatchers, a visit here is a rite of spring. An astonishing concentration of American cultural icons is buried here, including Henry Wadsworth Longfellow, Mary Baker Eddy (who was supposedly buried with her telephone), Winslow Homer, Buckminster Fuller, Fannie Farmer, and Bernard Malamud. In the spring, wandering the beautifully manicured paths of this lush and vibrant glade is truly an affirmation of life.

Downtown
and
North End

"One if by land, and two if by sea . . ."
—Henry Wadsworth Longfellow, "Paul Revere's Ride"

Essential Information for Walk Four

Length of walk:	2.6 miles
Terrain:	flat with one short hill
Time:	3 ½ hours at a leisurely pace, without going inside any of the buildings
This walk may be divided in two:	End first walk after Blackstone Block (approximately 2 hours)
Nearest T stop:	Park Street on Red and Green Lines
Starting point:	Exit T and walk on Tremont Street past Park Street Church to Old Granary Burying Ground

Supplements to the Walk

Highly Recommended

National Park Service talk in Faneuil Hall's Great Assembly Hall (on second floor)

Time:	15 minutes
Hours:	daily, 9:00 A.M.–4:30 P.M., every half-hour
Telephone:	617-242-5642
Admission:	free
When:	second third of walk at Faneuil Hall

Tour of Paul Revere House

Time:	35 minutes
Hours:	Apr. 15–Oct. 31: 9:30 A.M.– 5:15 P.M.; Nov. 1–Apr. 14: 9:30 A.M.–4:15 P.M.; closed major holidays and Mon. in Jan.–Mar.
Telephone:	617-523-2338
Admission:	$3.50; discount for seniors, students, and children
When:	last third of walk at North Square

Old North Church

Time:	15 minutes
Hours:	daily, Jun.–Oct.: 9:00 A.M.–6:00 P.M.; daily, Nov.–Dec.: 10:00 A.M. –5:00 P.M.; Tues.–Sun., Jan.–Feb.: 10:00 A.M.–4:00 P.M.; daily, Mar.–May: 9:00 A.M.–5:00 P.M.
Telephone:	617-523-6676
Admission:	free
When:	last third of walk on Salem Street

Lunch and stroll through North End

Of Further Interest

Old South Meeting House

Time:	20 minutes
Hours:	daily, Apr.–Oct.: 9:30 A.M.– 5:00 P.M.; daily, Nov.–Mar.: 10:00 A.M.–4:00 P.M.
Telephone:	617-482-6439
Admission:	$5; discount for seniors, students, and children
When:	first third of walk on Washington Street

Old State House

Time:	30 minutes
Hours:	daily, Sept.–Dec. and Feb.–Jun.: 9:00 A.M.–5:00 P.M.; daily, Jan.: 9:00 A.M.–4:00 P.M.; daily, Jul.– Aug.: 9:00 A.M.–6:00 P.M.
Telephone:	617-720-3290
Admission:	$5; discount for seniors, students, and children
When:	first third of walk on State Street

Downtown and North End - Walk Four

1. Old Granary Burying Ground
2. Boston Athenaeum
3. King's Chapel
4. School Street sidewalk mosaic
5. Old City Hall
6. Parker House Hotel
7. Old Corner Bookstore site
8. Irish Famine Memorial
9. Old South Meeting House
10. Spring Lane
11. Winthrop Building
12. Exchange Place
13. Site of Boston Massacre—Old State House
14. City Hall
15. Sears Crescent
16. Custom House
17. Dock Square
18. Faneuil Hall
19. Quincy Market
20. Statues of James Michael Curley
21. Holocaust Memorial
22. Union Oyster House
23. Blackstone Block—Boston Stone
24. Paul Revere House—Pierce-Hichborn House
25. North Square
26. Saint Stephen's Church
27. Paul Revere Mall—The Prado
28. Old North Church
29. Copp's Hill
30. #44 Hull Street

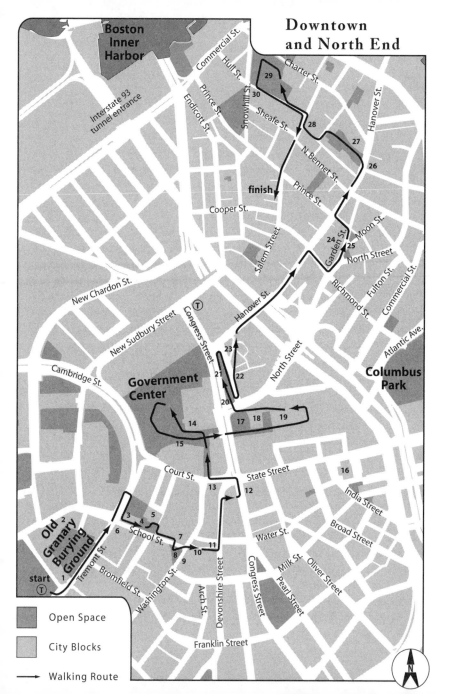

Downtown and North End

Boston Inner Harbor

Interstate 93 tunnel entrance

Commercial St.
Hull St.
Prince St.
Endicott St.
Snowhill St.
Sheafe St.
Charter St.
N. Bennet St
Hanover St.
Cooper St.
finish
Prince St.
Salem Street
Garden St.
Moon St.
North Street
Fulton St.
Commercial St.
New Chardon St.
Richmond St.
New Sudbury Street
Congress Street
Hanover St.
North Street
Columbus Park
Atlantic Ave.
Cambridge St.
Government Center
India Street
Court St.
State Street
Broad Street
Old Granary Burying Ground
Tremont St.
School St.
Washington St.
Devonshire Street
Arch St.
Congress Street
Water St.
Milk St.
Oliver Street
Pearl Street
start
Bromfield St.
Franklin Street

Legend

Open Space

City Blocks

→ Walking Route

N

There was a crooked man,
and he went a crooked mile,
And found a crooked sixpence
against a crooked stile,
He bought a crooked cat,
which caught a crooked mouse,
And they all lived together
in a little crooked house.

—Mother Goose

Men both crooked and virtuous will be celebrated in this meandering walk around Mother Goose's old neighborhood. Her domain was, and still is, the core of Boston, a city once so small that everyone walked from home, to tavern, to market, and to church. The layout of streets that seems illogical now made sense then; their curves and arbitrary endings accommodated trees, boulders, and streams. Despite outward sprawl, despite changes in topography and architecture, downtown is still the heart of the municipality, and the North End still embodies small-town community life. Among 20th-century skyscrapers, Boston has preserved its history—telling its stories through cherished landmarks and cemeteries. To visit them chronologically would require turning back on our path innumerable times, so fittingly, we will jump "higgledy-piggledy" from century to century, like Mother Goose's black hen.

❗❗
Enter and explore
cemetery

Boston is the only major American city to have five cemeteries within its commercial district—a revealing glimpse into the history of the original town. The **Old Granary Burying Ground [1],** the first of three to be visited, is occupied by an illustrious group of patriots, poets, politicians, and printers—at least 12,000 of them. This number appears unlikely until you understand the method of burial; bodies were often stacked four deep, not in caskets but wrapped in linen cloth and sprinkled with lime. They were placed facing east, enabling them to rise up facing the sun on Judgment Day. Graves were like beds, with headstones and footstones; inscriptions faced out so they could be read without trampling on the dead. The earliest of these, dating from the

Grave markers in
Old Granary
Burying Ground

1660s, reflect the Puritans' fire-and-brimstone feelings concerning death—macabre skulls and crossbones. Later carvings of the 18th and 19th centuries reflect a more benign view of the afterlife—cherubs, sheaves of wheat, classical urns, and willows.

The burying ground was filled by 1738, but bodies were added until 1879, when it was officially closed by the board of health. Gravestones were placed in random but congenial groupings until a 19th-century sexton decided to neaten things up, placing the stones in orderly rows. Commented Oliver Wendell Holmes: "Epitaphs were never famous for truth, but the old reproach of 'Here lies' never had such a wholesome illustration as in these outraged burial places, where the stone does lie above and the bones do not lie beneath."

The famous occupants are easy to spot as you stroll around this tranquil space. The list reads like a primer of the American Revolution: John Hancock, James Otis, Samuel Adams, Robert Treat Paine, and, of course, Paul Revere. Ben Franklin is buried in Philadelphia, but his parents are here, honored by a large obelisk with an epitaph written by their son, extolling their hard labor, honesty, piety, prudence, and virtue.

None of the latter qualities seems to have deterred the grave robbers who allegedly cut off and absconded with the famous hand of John Hancock on the night he was buried in 1793. His body followed suit, when, during 19th-century construction, someone made off with the rest of him.

Although no one made off with her body, there are still questions about the final resting place of a much-beloved Puritan, Mother [Elizabeth] Goose. The grave of her predecessor, Mary, the first wife of Isaac Vergoose, can be found in the far right corner. It is assumed that other members of the family lie here as well. Father Goose became a widower with 10 children at age 55, married Elizabeth, and fathered 10 more. Elizabeth, now mother to 20 children ("There was an old woman who lived in a shoe . . ."), moved into her jingle-writing phase, possibly to maintain her sanity. The jingles continued as the grandchildren began to proliferate. When Elizabeth became a widow, she moved in with her daughter, son-in-law, and their 14 children. She became a published poet when her daughter's husband, an impoverished printer, realized the charm of her songs and rhymes. He became wealthy on *Mother Goose's Melodies for Children,* and she became history—possibly a legend. This delightful story is hypothetical; neither the believers nor the debunkers seem to have proof positive concerning the originality of her rhymes.

The cemetery's name reflects the historical proximity of a granary. Other neighboring buildings included an almshouse, a prison, and a workhouse. The land was occasionally rented for grazing; bulls, cows, and pigs shared space with some of America's premier Puritans.

Today the surrounding real estate is much more valuable: adjoining the Old Granary Burying Ground is the exclusive **Boston Athenaeum [2],**

Note 5-story brick building abutting back of cemetery

founded by the city's pure-bred literati. This private library, established in 1803, also has its famous ghosts. Was the soul of the Reverend Thaddeus Mason Harris en route to the cemetery when it encountered author Nathaniel Hawthorne in the Athenaeum? On the day of Harris's death, Hawthorne found him seated in his usual place: "In the reading room of the Athenaeum conversation is strictly forbidden, and I could not have addressed the apparition without drawing instant notice and indignant frowns of the slumberous old gentlemen around me. I myself, too, at that time, was as shy as any ghost, and followed the ghost's rule never to speak first." Although decorum and propriety may be the operative words for this library, it owns a rare 18th-century autobiography of a convicted highwayman, bound in his own skin!

‼

Leave cemetery; walk left on Tremont Street and cross School Street; stop on far corner across from church

Whereas the Old Granary Burying Ground represents a "who's who" of those who founded this country, **King's Chapel [3]** represented a "who's who" of those who fled to England. This was the first house of worship for Boston's Anglican community. The Puritans immigrated to America to escape the Church of England; by 1688, however, the colony was ruled by a royal governor. He wanted a church where he could worship as he had back home, so he peremptorily used his power of eminent domain to claim land that the Puritans had refused to sell. This was *the* society church before the Revolution; its first parishioners were the most aristocratic of the colonists. When war broke out, over half of the congregation, including their rector, left with the British fleet. Some Anglicans remained, loyal to their theology but not to the Crown. In a breach of practice they ordained a new minister themselves, rather than sending him to England for investiture. This action resulted in a virtual excommunication from the Anglican community. The congregation eventually redefined rites and rules, becoming the first Unitarian Church in America.

The royal governor's original wooden structure was replaced in 1754 by this august edifice designed by architect Peter Harrison of Newport, Rhode Island. Harrison rivaled Charles Bulfinch (see Beacon Hill Walk) as America's first major architect. In a remarkable testimony to his skill, he designed the church without ever seeing the site: plans and specs were negotiated by mail. Construction lasted four years, during which time the parishioners continued to worship inside the old church while the new one grew up around it. When the building was complete, the old church was dismantled and thrown out the windows of the new one. Unfortunately, the congregation could not afford to finish the building as envisioned by Harrison. They managed to add a front portico several decades later but never completed the steeple, thus giving the building its rather cumbersome shape. The massive 25-foot columns are superb by-products of the tight budget—they are crafted of wood (plentiful and cheap in New England) and disguised as granite to match the rest of the building.

But in the 18th century, this building still represented the official Church of England, and when it was dedicated in 1754, the crowd of colonists

Cross Tremont Street to King's Chapel Burying Ground

greeted it with missiles of garbage, manure, and dead animals. The Crown had appropriated part of the **adjacent burying ground** for its congregants, and the locals neither forgave nor forgot. This, the first cemetery in Boston, was the resting place for all the early Puritans. One of the more notorious, Elizabeth Pain (damned as an adulteress), was said to be the model for Hawthorne's best-known character, Hester Prynne. As we know from his experience in the Athenaeum, Hawthorne was intrigued by ghosts, and he often wandered here, seeking inspiration.

The bodies below must have turned over in their—or others'—graves when they heard that the neighborhood had gone to the Anglicans. However, that whooshing sound you hear is not the admonishing voices of Puritans, but the sound of the subway emanating from the ventilation shaft, which, in some unsettling way, complements the design of the cemetery.

: :

Return to School Street; turn left; stop at sidewalk mosaic in front of Old City Hall

By contrast, **School Street** represents the city very much alive. Boston's commitment to education began on this appropriately named thoroughfare. Here stood America's first public school, Boston Latin, founded in 1635 (more than a year before Harvard) and open to any (male) child. The school is celebrated by Lilli Ann Rosenberg's 1983 **sidewalk mosaic [4],** her interpretation of an early American teaching mnemonic. Boston Latin, now located near the Fenway, is still a premier public high school, and yes, it is coed. Its illustrious alums fill Boston history and this book: Cotton Mather, Sam Adams, Charles Bulfinch, Phillips Brooks,

Henry Lee Higginson, and Charles William Eliot.

Enter Old City Hall courtyard

Two of Boston Latin's most famous students flank one of Boston's most illustrious buildings. On the left stands a sculpture of **Ben Franklin** created by Richard S. Greenough in 1855. The bronze reliefs at the base of this sculpture depict four significant facets of Franklin's career: printer, scientist, revolutionary, and diplomat. Author George Weston Jr. quotes a contemporary analysis of the statue: "Richard Greenough ... once told me that in studying for the statue he found the left side of the great man's face philosophical and reflective and the right side, funny and smiling. You will find that Greenough so delineated it. Viewed from the east one sees Franklin the statesman; from the west, the author of 'Poor Richard's Almanac.'"

On the right stands **Josiah Quincy,** an early-19th-century mayor of Boston and president of Harvard. His impact on the city was profound. A visionary, he redefined the services government should provide for citizens. His courtly bearing belied his compassion for the common man. You will meet him again at the market that bears his name.

Although these gentlemen represented the New World and a new country, they still spoke the King's English. It is doubtful their ears would have been attuned to today's Boston accent. What would they have made of the familiar, "Hi-hahwahya?" ("Hi, how are you?"), the typical greeting shared by politicians at City Hall?

The **Old City Hall [5],** designed by Gridley J. F. Bryant and Arthur Gilman (see Back Bay Walk), was built from 1862 to 1865 in the French Empire style, which these architects introduced to America. Nicknamed the "Parisian Wedding Cake," it is universally described as exuberant, with its over-the-top inclusion of every architectural trick in the book. The architects have taken the standard Empire characteristics—mansard roof, dormer windows, significant central section, and square tower, and iced their cake with dentils, pilasters, brackets, keystones, columns, and arches. They aspired to create "the most elaborate and conspicuous" new building. According to architectural critic Donlyn Lyndon, "The French hardly ever made it as well," observing that the relationship among the design elements is perfect in scale. A dissenting opinion comes from Edwin O'Connor in *The Last Hurrah,* his novel based on Mayor James Michael Curley, perhaps this building's most famous occupant. He called it "a lunatic pile of a building; a great, grim, resolutely ugly, dust catcher." In 1969, city government moved to a larger, more modern space; their former, more flamboyant quarters now house private offices and, for many years, hosted Boston's premier French restaurant.

👣
Look back up
School Street to
Parker House Hotel

But in the mid–19th century, "foodies" flocked to the **Parker House Hotel [6]** across the street. The life of its founder, farm boy Harvey Parker, is the quintessential American success story. In 1825 he arrived in Boston from Maine with less than one dollar to his name; he died 60 years later, a millionaire. He dreamed of being a hotelier while working as a groom, a coachman, and a café owner. "Location, location, location" was his good fortune—his hotel was situated between the seats of state and city government. Nevertheless, his remarkable food and hospitality accounted for the loyalty of his clientele. His was the first hotel to offer round-the-clock gourmet dining; his French chef was paid ten times the going rate. Parker House rolls and Boston cream pie, both made famous here, are still classics on menus across the country. The city's signature main dish, Boston scrod, is not a species of fish, but rather the finest, youngest whitefish catch of the day—named and served here.

The famous and the infamous called the Parker House home—from Dickens to Hopalong Cassidy to Joan Crawford to burlesque queens. James Michael Curley and JFK launched campaigns here. And before they launched major political movements, Ho Chi Minh and Malcolm X had menial jobs here. Yet the apex of the Parker House as a cultural cynosure occurred in the 19th century. The literati of greater Boston met here monthly for a seven-course meal of glorious food and intellectual confabulation. Called the Saturday Club, its members included Emerson, Longfellow, Holmes, Whittier, and their publisher, Jamie Fields. The latter introduced Charles Dickens to the group. The British writer's appeal was that of Mick Jagger today, and Dickens too was a peacock, outrageously dressed in colorful coat, boots, matching cravat, hat, and gloves. When Dickens was in Boston on tour, a bodyguard was posted at his door to protect him from adoring fans who wanted a glimpse of him rehearsing the animated facial expressions and gestures he used to create characters in his readings. He evidently protected himself from his fans with his favorite "jug anglice." Holmes observed, "No witch at her incantation could be more rapt in her task than Dickens was at his as he stooped over the drink he was mixing"—an English gin punch, with an emphasis on the gin.

Cross and continue down School Street; sit in plaza in front of Borders Bookstore

Two hundred years earlier, in this Puritan settlement, witches' incantations were more to be feared than imbibed. In 1630, Governor John Winthrop and his intrepid band of 900 came here to the Shawmut Peninsula from nearby Charlestown, which had contaminated water and bothersome "Woolves, Rattle-snakes and Musketos." The settlers called their new home Boston, after the English town of the same name. It is hard to visualize the small 17th-century homes and shops, orchards and cornfields, in the midst of this 21st-century cacophony. Down the street from Governor Winthrop lived John Cogan, the town's first merchant, who sold "tobacco, clothing and crooked-lane ware." Nearby was Mrs. Sherman, a favorite subject of the rumor mill churning at the town pump. She kept a boarder and a pig, both of which caused trouble. It was suggested that she granted "favors" to the boarder; her pig wound up in the oven of Captain Keayne, the pound keeper, who swore in court it was his own to eat. Right in the middle lived Samuel Cole, proprietor of the town tavern. Cogan married the widow Winthrop, Cole married the widow Keayne—Mrs. Sherman probably did not marry—and it was all executed with Puritan rectitude.

Although Salem is infamous for witch trials, Boston has the dubious distinction of being the first town in New England to hang a convicted witch—Margaret Jones in 1648. Puritan life in Boston rigidly adhered to the rules set forth by theology and doctrine. Punishable transgressions were too numerous to recount or even remember, but among them were: "eavesdropping, meddling, naughty speeches, neglecting work, pulling hair, pushing his wife, repeating a scandalous lie, scolding, selling dear, selling strong water by small measure, sleeping in a meeting, spying into the chamber of his master and mistress and reporting what he saw." Hanging was the punishment for being a murderer, a Quaker, or a witch. Stocks, pillories, ear-cropping, nose-slitting, branding, and public whipping were the penalties for minor sins.

Damned if you did, damned if you didn't. The carpenter who crafted the first stocks was the first to be confined in them—for charging too much for his work. A returning sea captain was whipped for publicly kissing his wife on the sabbath; one year later he was again publicly chastised for "neglecting his wife and living apart from her." Alice Thomas was exiled for being a "common baud" and giving her customers "opportunity to commit carnall wickedness." She, however, figured out the system: she made a big donation toward the building of a municipal seawall and was allowed to return to town. And even if you did nothing at all, you were locked in church during services—lest you even thought of leaving.

Author George Weston Jr. wryly observes, "It was bad enough to be a Puritan in Boston Town, but

Note red-brick building at end of School Street

it was infinitely worse to be anything else. In spite of their pious talk of religious freedom, the first settlers were just as narrow and intolerant as the Lord Bishops who had forced them to leave England." The story of Anne Hutchinson, a respected midwife who was also an outspoken, independent thinker, shows the true colors of colonial leaders in church and state. Married to a successful merchant, she lived at this site. Her future nemesis, Governor Winthrop, lived across the street. The reigning churchmen felt threatened when her women's discussion groups grew, attracting men as well. But it wasn't just the number of her followers that upset the church hierarchy—it was her antinomian philosophy, the belief that the Holy Spirit exists in each individual and that good works lead to salvation. This rather cut the clergy out of the loop.

The Reverend John Cotton, fearing his former acolyte would preempt him, declared her weekly meetings to be a "promiscuous and filthie coming together of men and women without Distinction of Relation of Marriage" and judged her ideas harshly: "Your opinions frett like a gangrene and spread like a leprosie, and will eate out the very Bowells of Religion." She was banished in 1637 and, accompanied by family and 60 followers, fled to more tolerant Rhode Island. After her husband died in 1642 she moved to New York, where tragically, she and 14 of her children were massacred by Indians. Governor Winthrop mused in his journal that Hutchinson's downfall was caused by her intellectual life. She should have stuck to homemaking and left the thinking to men, "whose minds are stronger."

Two hundred and twenty years later, in the mid–19th century, this very site became the center of liberal thinking in New England. Here at the **Old Corner Bookstore [7],** entrepreneur Jamie Fields reigned, shepherding his famous flock of writers—publishing, humoring, and promoting them. He and his partner, George Ticknor, were the preeminent publishers of the day, Jamie in the public eye, George managing the money. Their roster included American authors Emerson, Longfellow, Thoreau, Holmes, and Harriet Beecher Stowe, as well as British writers Thackeray, Browning, Tennyson, and Dickens. As observed in *Harper's Magazine,* the Old Corner Bookstore orbit was a close, influential one, "the exchange of wit, the Rialto of current good things, the hub of the Hub." Jamie's ability to spot an author was legendary, but at least once he was misguided by a bias similar to John Winthrop's. When Louisa May Alcott showed him her writing, he urged her not to give up her day job as a teacher. In fact, he loaned her $40 to buy classroom supplies, remarking that she could pay him back if she ever became successful. She honored her debt . . .

For others in the mid–19th century, the Hub played a different role. Fleeing the potato famine, the first wave of desperate and destitute Irish, over 37,000 of them, arrived in Boston in 1847. Robert Shure's 1998 **Irish Famine Memorial [8]** commemorates the travails of their life in Ireland and their optimism for building a new life in America. In the land of opportunity, however, Irish immigrants faced new adversity—prejudice. In reaction to this huge influx of newcomers, who were both

Note sculpture in middle of plaza

poor and Catholic, a new political party arose in Boston. Secret handshakes and passwords were badges of party membership—the underlying philosophy was to eliminate "Rome, Rum, and Robbery," replacing them with "Temperance, Liberty, and Protestantism." The American Party, dedicated to protecting the nation from foreigners, succeeded for a short time. Its members quickly rose to fill the major political offices in the state, and its power spread south along the eastern seaboard. Familiarly and ironically called the "Know Nothings" for refusing to discuss their clandestine activities, members made their purpose and prejudice clear. Their star fell in the mid-1850s as the nation faced an even greater threat—civil war. It took Boston 150 years to acknowledge the cultural importance of Irish immigration.

!!
Look across Washington Street to red-brick Old South Meeting House

The **Old South Meeting House [9],** now a museum, waited for more than 100 years for frugal Bostonians to ackowledge its historical preeminence. This venerable building looks very much as it did in the 18th century. Typical of Puritan ecclesiastical style, the church is simple and unembellished, with clear glass windows. Its outstanding architectural feature is a lofty spire, long an integral part of the downtown landscape. This unadorned building reflects the Puritan belief that an ornate and richly decorated church interfered with man's relationship to God. Sunday services could last up to six hours and were monitored by a large hourglass that was flipped as the sand interminably passed through.

In addition to serving as a house of worship, Old South also accommodated large municipal meetings. The Boston Tea Party, the colonists' most well-known and colorful protest against British taxation, began here. History books describe a rowdy assembly of over 5,000 men who convened on December 16, 1773, to decide how to deal with the most recent offensive English tax. Should you go inside, try to imagine how this building could possibly accommodate so many—its capacity today is only 650. But it is no exaggeration to state that on that night an angry and resolute crowd marched from the church to the waterfront and dumped all the English tea into the harbor. British revenge took the form of desecration; in the early days of the Revolutionary War soldiers turned Old South into an indoor riding arena, ripping out pews and destroying books and artifacts.

After the war the building served once more as a house of worship; then, in the late 19th century, its congregation moved uptown (see Back Bay Walk). Used for a variety of purposes thereafter, Old South was ultimately threatened with demolition, but in a pattern often repeated in Boston, a priceless historical treasure was saved by the ladies. In 1877, philanthropist Mary Hemenway rallied her friends, "especially from better families," to organize fairs, balls, auctions, and readings by famous authors to raise funds for its preservation. Historian Walter Muir Whitehill admiringly applauded the effort, "the first instance in Boston where respect for the historical and architectural heritage of the city triumphed over considerations of profit, expediency, laziness, and vulgar convenience."

Nothing about this narrow, shadowed alley hints at its critical importance in the early 17th cen-

Cross Washington Street; walk left to Spring Lane; turn right

tury. Here stood the spring that quenched the thirst of a robust community; no vestige of the water remains other than a **plaque placed halfway down the alley [10]** on the left. Although the spring dried up as the settlement grew and people dug their own wells, it surprisingly gushed again in 1869 during the construction of the post office at the bottom of the lane.

Exit Spring Lane; cross diagonally to corner of Water and Devonshire Streets; look back at green-and-rust office building

The **Winthrop Building [11],** #276–#278 Washington Street, with its sensuous shape and strong colors, is ironically named after Puritan governor John Winthrop; it is doubtful he would have approved. In 1893, avant-garde architect Clarence H. Blackall experimented with materials and shapes to create a curvilinear narrow profile on a steel skeleton. The most coveted interior space in this nine-story structure is on this end, where the building is only one bay wide, allowing light in from three sides. The exquisite decoration, the moldings, the bas-relief ornamentation, and the terra-cotta banding are remarkable. This singular treasure dares to be different among its conservative Bostonian street-mates.

Walk right on Devonshire Street; turn right down alley across from Visitor's Center; cross Congress Street to glass skyscraper

An interesting architectural marriage has resulted from a capitalist-conservationist "pre-nup" at **Exchange Place [12].** Developers in the mid-1980s agreed to maintain part of the façade and the interior of the 19th-century stock exchange that stood on this valuable site. The most striking aspect of this accommodation is the grand and opulent double stairway that dramatically prevails in the five-story glass atrium of an otherwise sterile downtown skyscraper.

A horrendous event took place 200 feet away and 200 years earlier. Like the Boston Tea Party, the **Boston Massacre [13]** was another crucial event in the colonies' inexorable march toward war with England. On a cold and snowy March evening in 1770, a minor altercation between a British soldier and a young apprentice escalated. The Bostonian taunted the redcoat, who, provoked and irritated, cuffed the lad with his musket. A crowd gathered; more redcoats rushed to the scene. During the melee, the bells of Old South began to toll; their pealing was often a signal for fire. Chaos erupted, someone yelled "fire," and the British responded. Eight colonists were shot; three died immediately, and two more died later. Not surprisingly, there were at least two sides to this story. Patriot Paul Revere used the event to mythologize the colonists' oppression with a widely circulated engraving entitled, *The Bloody Massacre Perpetrated on King Street*. Depicting British soldiers in battle formation, firing their muskets at innocent young men, it became an incendiary tool for revolution. Yet John Adams, also a fervent patriot, agreed to defend the soldiers in court, despite potential damage to his reputation. He proved that the tragedy resulted from confusion and that the British officer in charge had never ordered his men to shoot. His case was so strong and so well argued that his reputation emerged intact. The redcoats, although exonerated of this offense, were still considered the enemy.

The **Old State House [13]** has housed both monarchists and rebels. The oldest public build-

With your back to Exchange Place, turn right and walk on Congress Street to corner of State Street; cross to triangle in middle of intersection

Note red-brick building with balcony overlooking State Street

ing in Boston, it was built in 1713 on a site that had already served as the town center for 80 years, a crossroads of commerce and politics. The State Street side (formerly King Street) looked down to the harbor, which at the time was much closer; the opposite Washington Street side (formerly Cornhill) faced the land route to the west. Here all kinds of transactions occurred: merchants and sea captains met downstairs to discuss trade and finance; government officials carried on the business of state upstairs; the ladies met outside to trade in the business of society.

The prominent balcony of the Old State House witnessed three spectacular historic events. On July 18, 1776, the county sheriff read the Declaration of Independence (ratified two weeks earlier in Philadelphia) to a euphoric crowd. In a frenzy of patriotism the British lion and unicorn, symbolizing the power of the oppressors, were torn from the gable and burned in celebratory bonfires. King Street became State Street in honor of the new republic.

In the fall of 1789, President George Washington returned to Boston, his first visit since the early days of the Revolution (see Cambridge Walk). Throngs of cheering tradesmen lined his route from the outskirts to the center of town. Each group, from candle makers to shipbuilders, carried its own identifying white flag and parted as the great man passed by on his white stallion. Alas, one key player was missing—Governor John Hancock. He arrogantly believed that here, in his state, his rank was highest, and hence he waited for the president to call on him. Washington thought otherwise, and although convinced to enter the city, he was clearly offended by Hancock's breach of etiquette. Emissaries were sent to the governor, who was finally persuaded of his *faux pas*. He had his legs wrapped in bandages, claimed to have been felled by a bad case of gout, and was received at the State House by a doubting but gracious president. After Washington's departure, every neighborhood petitioned to name a street in his honor; town and state officials worked together to create the longest thoroughfare in the Commonwealth, which now runs from here to Rhode Island.

Ironically, in 1976 the reigning British monarch, Queen Elizabeth, was the guest of honor at America's bicentennial celebration in Boston. She addressed the cheering crowd flanked by replicas of the lion and the unicorn, now restored to their places of honor. Her well wishes were delivered from the very spot where the Declaration of Independence had been read 200 years earlier.

Like the Old South Meeting House, the Old State House had been threatened with demolition in the late 19th century. It took a city lacking a colonial past to make Boston appreciate its own. When Chicago offered to buy this historical gem, locals realized its importance and raised the funds to maintain it as a museum. Having survived fires, commercial rehabs, and total disrepair, the building you see has its original exterior walls, an 1830 interior, an 1882 tower, 1909 doors, and a 20th-century roof and sundial.

Cross to State House; walk straight ahead, keeping Old State House on your left; at corner, cross State Street to pedestrian mall; walk up steps and turn left to center of large City Hall Plaza

City Hall at
Government
Center

One wonders if, 150 years from now, a movement
will form to save the current **Government
Center,** a model of 1960s Brutalist architecture
that houses federal, state, and municipal offices.
This controversial and provocative development
redefined a whole neighborhood. The old Scollay
Square it replaced was gritty; home to tenements,
pubs, strip joints, tattoo parlors, and bordellos.
Sailors, traveling salesmen, and college boys spent
their salaries, bonuses, and allowances here.
Though derelict, at least it had personality. In the
words of architectural historian Donlyn Lyndon,

"As a layout it [Government Center] has no character, an aimless set of streets that wander disconsolately among high and alien buildings, with only the barest traces of a previous world and lots of evidence of the 1960s."

For it was during this era that Mayor John Collins, Boston redevelopment director Ed Logue, and artistic director I. M. Pei redesigned this neighborhood of shadowy lanes and alleys. Creating open space on such a scale in an urban downtown setting was novel and exciting. The resulting complex is monumental, but to many it is off-putting. Looming over the windy empty plaza is the award-winning **City Hall [14],** designed by the team of Kallman, McKinnell & Knowles. An outstanding example of Brutalism, a style popularized by Le Corbusier in the 1950s, it is constructed of *beton brut*—"concrete in the raw." Form follows function: the offices of the mayor and the city council are situated on the middle floors between their public and private roles; large ceremonial rooms are on the ground level; multiple bureaucratic cubicles take up the top levels (note how the repetitive small windows delineate the latter). It is a forceful architectural statement.

Opinions can be forceful as well. Architectural critic Tom Fletcher observes, "The fun of Brutalism is imagining the building as a heavily muscled, thick-fingered, knuckle-dragging, semi-monstrous intransigent brute with a slow stupid stare. (This one has numerous deeply hooded square eyesockets—scary!)" On the other hand, former *New York Times* critic Ada Louise Huxtable sees something more profound: "What has been gained is a notable achievement in the creation and control of urban space, and in the uses of monumentality and humanity in the best pattern of great city building." Yet when then-mayor John Collins first saw the design he gasped and someone in the room exclaimed, "what the hell is that?" Paradoxically, in 1976, under the aegis of the American Institute of Architects, a poll of historians and architects voted it the sixth greatest American building in history. By contrast, in 2008 it topped VirtualTourist.com's list of the World's Top 10 Ugliest Buildings and Monuments.

Huxtable continues, "Old and new Boston are joined through an act of urban design that relates directly to the quality of the city and its life." Boston strives to reconcile the new with the historical, and Government Center honors the past. **Sears Crescent [15]**, the curving red-brick 19th-century block of buildings that flanks City Hall, was purposely incorporated into the master plan. A whimsical **copper tea kettle** saved from Scollay Square hangs at its corner. Cast in 1874 to draw customers to the Oriental Tea Company, the teapot was unveiled with great fanfare. A prize of 40 pounds of tea was offered to the person who could guess the volume of the giant kettle. Thirteen thousand contestants gathered to hear who had won. The liquid capacity proved to be 227 gallons, 2 quarts, 1 pint, and 3 gills . . . eight winners shared the bounty. But no one guessed that the kettle could also accommodate eight boys plus a man in a silk top hat. To the crowd's delight, they emerged from the pot one by one, a human tempest in a teapot.

!!

Look for huge
suspended teapot
at end of Sears
Crescent

Walk along right side of City Hall; stop at top of stairs; note Custom House tower in skyline to your right

It is hard to conceive that the beautiful **Custom House [16]** tower that graces the skyline was once as reviled as the Hancock Tower in Back Bay (see Back Bay Walk). But like the Hancock, when it was built, Bostonians resented the new silhouette. In 1915 this 495-foot-high, 29-story tower, with its identifying clock, rose up alongside the warehouses of the harbor. It was erected despite a city height restriction of 125 feet; its owner, the federal government, did not feel bound by municipal law. Bostonians were aghast at Washington's cavalier attitude toward the waterfront panorama; equally upsetting was that civil servants in Washington fused an Italianate tower onto the classic Greek Revival Custom House. Yet over time locals have come to be justifiably proud of this maritime landmark, now recycled as a luxurious Marriott time-share accommodation.

Walk down stairs behind City Hall; cross Congress Street to statue of Sam Adams in plaza in front of Faneuil Hall

In 1800, the Custom House, now a block from the sea, was once so close to the boats in the harbor, one could practically touch their bowsprits from its windows. In 1700, **Dock Square [17],** where you are now standing, was the harbor; the undulating line scratched into the surrounding sidewalk shows the ancient watermark. This landfill provided much-needed space for a growing community; by the mid-18th century it numbered over 3,000 homes and 300 shops. As the community grew and matured, the somber Puritan ethos became diluted. "I saw not one prude while I was there," reported a delighted visitor from the South.

Typical of this new breed of Bostonian was *bon vivant* Peter Faneuil. Generous, entrepreneurial, and extremely wealthy, he visualized a more modern metropolis. Anticipating the commercial advantage of creating a permanent central marketplace and the need for a large town-meeting space, he offered to underwrite such a community structure. Despite Faneuil's civic-minded generosity, the proposal was barely endorsed by the town council; many merchants lobbied against the new idea, fearing competition, regulation, and change. A permanent structure would have threatened the freedom of their transient pushcart business. However, once the concept was implemented in 1742, **Faneuil Hall [18],** with its merchant stalls on the first floor and town-meeting space above, became an immediate success. Alas, Peter Faneuil died six months later of too much high life; yet his legacy lives on—no matter how you pronounce his name. The name etched on his tomb is *Funel;* his French Huguenot relatives probably identified themselves as *Feh-noy;* Bostonians today call him *Fan-el* or *Fan-yuhl.*

Two visionaries: Faneuil conceptualized a new approach to commerce, and **Samuel Adams** conceived a new nation. This revolutionary activist is celebrated in front of the building where he made many of his fiery speeches. After Harvard, he went into the family business, a brewery. But microbreweries were not yet chic; his went flat, and so he tried politics. His first elected office was tax collector in 1756; he was so inefficient that he was reelected nine times by his appreciative constituents. His true talent, however, was inspirational rhetoric. It was Adams who rallied the colonists to rebel against detested British taxation, thus becoming one of America's founding fathers.

Faneuil Hall

Home to the impassioned revolutionary oratory delivered by Adams and his compatriots, Faneuil Hall was soon designated the "Cradle of Liberty." Yet at the same time the British also utilized the facility. While attending General Burgogne's farce, *The Blockade of Boston,* soldiers and loyalists were rocked right out of the cradle. Midperformance, an actor exclaimed, "The Yankees are marching on Bunker Hill!" The audience loved the humor until they realized that the actor was serious—and the rebels were no longer a joke.

Thirty years later Faneuil Hall had become a thoroughly American institution and, like the country, needed more room. In 1805 Boston's renowned architect Charles Bulfinch (see Beacon Hill Walk), was commissioned to renovate the space. The structure he designed remained true to the spirit of the 1742 original but was enhanced by doubling the width and adding a third floor. Bulfinch's classical vocabulary is subtle and dignified. The building appears symmetrical and balanced, yet each story is taller than the one below it, creating an illusion of great height.

Poised atop the cupola is a grasshopper. Thirty-eight pounds in weight, over 4 feet long, with green glass doorknobs for eyes, he has survived in this spot since 1742. The creature was probably copied from the vane that graced the Royal Exchange in London—its symbolic meaning, if any was meant, has long been lost. Nevertheless, the grasshopper acquired significance to Bostonians, especially during the War of 1812, when the question "What's on top of Faneuil Hall?" was asked of all strangers entering the city. Those who did not know the answer were suspected as spies.

And should they be spies, they would likely be dealt with by the Ancient and Honorable Artillery Company of Massachusetts. Still housed in Faneuil Hall, their artifacts reflect America's military history; they have participated in every engagement since the Revolution. The Great Assembly Hall, on the second level, has resounded with the words of America's distinguished orators, from Samuel Adams to William Lloyd Garrison to John F. Kennedy. Today, National Park rangers animate the Assembly Hall every half hour on the hour. Their 20-minute talk is highly recommended.

!!
Walk to opposite side of Faneuil Hall; enter through center doors; walk upstairs to second floor

Exiting Faneuil Hall, facing the monumental **Quincy Market [19],** you may encounter jugglers, street musicians, mimes, and shoppers. Two hundred years ago, this upscale destination was another kettle of fish:

❗❗

Walk along right side of Quincy Market; cut through building under center dome; turn left and meander back toward Congress Street

A jostling mass of people making their way among butchers cutting their meat in the Hall, vendors peddling their fruits and vegetables under wooden sheds along the outside walls, and fishmongers stationed behind long wooden benches lined with large tubs filled with all kinds of seafood. On "high market days," customers and pedestrians were in constant danger of being knocked down by stagecoaches or bowled over by droves of pigs being hustled to market.

In addition to the congestion in the market district, visitors were repelled by the abominable stench, combining the oily smells from the docks and the sickish odors of mud flats at low tide with the repulsive reek of uncollected street refuse and rotting garbage. The Town Dock, the pond directly behind Faneuil Hall, had become a stagnant receptacle for all kinds of filth and rubbish. In 1805 one member of the Night Watch recorded in his log book that the pond was full of "putrid fish and dead dogs and cats."

—Boston A to Z

Elected in 1823, Boston's farsighted mayor, Josiah Quincy (whose statue stands at Old City Hall), combined the qualities of developer, entrepreneur, and urban planner. Astride his horse, he toured his dominion every day at 5:00 A.M. As part of his sweeping reforms, "the Great Mayor" reorganized the city's health and fire departments, created infrastructure to improve the lives of the poor, hired the first garbage collectors and municipal street cleaners, laid sewers, and illuminated the streets. He drained the Town Dock and commissioned architect Alexander Parris to build the New Faneuil Hall Market. A grateful citizenry reelected him five times.

The New Faneuil Hall Market's name was soon changed to Quincy Market to honor the city's creative mayor. Parris designed a colossal but user-friendly Greek Revival market building, whose templelike exterior belies the bustling interior. Energy radiates from people buying and selling, filling the cavernous space with stimuli that vie for attention. Warehouses on either side (now converted to boutiques and eateries) were privately built but required to conform to Parris's vision.

The vision has waxed and waned. A 1940s guidebook advises that "you go through vegetable crates, plucked chickens, sides of beef, and the incredible clamor of the buying and selling of food. . . . It is as unattractive a spot as you will encounter." By the 1960s, the food markets had moved out of town and *The New York Times* characterized the area as "a small dingy, historic, and conspicuously empty stage." In the 1970s, developer Rouse and Company transformed the shabby marketplace into Boston's premier tourist attraction. Although skeptics thought that suburban malls had made downtown shopping obsolete, Rouse's renovation confounded their predictions; this revitalization became the prototype for downtown rehabs in Baltimore, New Orleans, and New York. Although decried by some locals as the kitsch capital of the city, natives, as well as tourists, still flock here for the restaurants, the shops, and "the scene." Vendors have become national ice cream chains and international clothiers; different vendors and different shoppers, but commerce still drives Faneuil Hall Marketplace.

Boston's celebrated **James Michael Curley** (see Beacon Hill Walk) was a slightly different sort of businessman. Holding a range of elected offices from 1900–1950, he was a product of the Irish political machine. His loyalty was renowned. While running for city alderman, he took the mail-carrier exam for a newly arrived countryman. When exposed and jailed for it, he maintained, "I did it for a friend," forever endearing himself to his constituency and winning the election. During his four terms as mayor, he taxed the rich and initiated projects to benefit the poor, simultaneously lining his own pockets. He lived in a mansion and vacationed on his yacht—despite a meager $10,000 annual salary. But his constituents saw the empathetic side of him: upon entering City Hall for the first time, he gathered all the scrubwomen, shook their hands, and promised them long-handled mops so they would never have to work on their knees again. This kind of largesse, coupled with the strategy of his machine ("Vote often and early for Curley!"), made him a legendary mayor, congressman, and governor. A complicated and fascinating character, he has been depicted in Edwin O'Connor's fictionalized account, *The Last Hurrah,* and Jack Beatty's biography, *The Rascal King.* This multifaceted man is celebrated by Lloyd Lillie's **two statues [20]:** the seated figure represents the

Cross North and Union Streets to small park

compassionate Curley; the standing figure portrays the charismatic orator.

Continue through center of park to Holocaust Memorial

The words of Holocaust survivor and Nobel Peace Prize winner Elie Wiesel quickly change the mood, from market bustle to contemplation: "Look at these towers, passerby, and try to imagine what they really mean—what they symbolize—what they evoke. They evoke an era of incommensurate darkness, an era in history when civilization lost its humanity and humanity its soul." Boston's **Holocaust Memorial [21]** is composed of six 54-foot glass-and-steel towers rising from a pit of black granite. Because the events and aftermath of the Holocaust represent unfathomable realities, architect Stanley Saitowitz resolutely designed a structure that invites different interpretations. The towers can be perceived as smokestacks of the death camps or, when illuminated at night, as candles honoring the dead. The number six is echoed: six towers, six million Jews killed, six major concentration camps. Etchings in glass and granite pay homage to the victims of the horrific tragedy: the glass is engraved with random numbers from one to six million; the granite is inscribed with moving quotations. Perhaps the most poignant and unsettling is the final quotation, which is attributed to Martin Niemoeller, a Lutheran pastor:

They came first for the Communists,
and I didn't speak up
because I wasn't a Communist.
Then they came for the Jews,
and I didn't speak up because I wasn't a Jew.

Then they came for the trade unionists,
and I didn't speak up
because I wasn't a trade unionist.
Then they came for the Catholics,
and I didn't speak up because I was a Protestant.
Then they came for me,
and by that time no one was left to speak up.

This 1995 memorial is purposely located along **Boston's Freedom Trail,** for it resonates with the principles of freedom for which the early patriots fought. The narrow red-brick path of the Freedom Trail is flanked by a granite border. It meanders down the sidewalk through colonial Boston, connecting 16 major historic sites. Over three million tourists annually become acquainted with America's Revolutionary War history as they stroll this three-mile route.

👣

Cross Union Street to Freedom Trail on sidewalk in front of Union Oyster House; peek inside

Opened in 1826, the **Union Oyster House [22]** has maintained its name since its inception, making it the oldest restaurant operating under the same name in the country. It has aged beautifully, and the oysters are still fresh. But its history goes back much further. It was built in 1714 as a residence; by the time of the Revolution it housed publisher Isaiah Thomas and his patriotic newspaper, *The Massachusetts Spy*. Right before the fighting began, Thomas managed to get the press to Worcester, from where he was able to publish the first account of the Battles of Lexington and Concord.

This aging warren, known as the **Blackstone Block [23]**, is architecturally most representative of colonial Boston. The mazelike cobbled

‼

Walk past Union
Oyster House down
alley to entrance of
Boston Stone Gift
Shop

streets are the last ones remaining from the early city. Once paved with seashells, the names— "Creek," "Marsh," and "Salt"—indicate how close they once were to the water. Both commercial and residential (stores downstairs, homes above), this neighborhood was home to Hancocks and Franklins. The famous **Boston Stone [23]** still dwells here. This 30-inch round piece of granite was brought from England in 1700 by a painter to grind his colors; some 30 years later it was embedded in a wall in imitation of the London Stone, from which all distances were measured. It is not clear that this marker was ever considered the center of Boston, but it was a landmark; contemporary newspapers cited stores as "near the Boston Stone" or "just west of the Boston Stone."

‼

Emerge on Hanover
Street; turn right;
cross Blackstone
Street/Surface
Road; continue into
the North End

Just east of the Boston Stone you enter the **North End.** A self-contained and unique part of Boston, it feels like a European enclave, with winding streets, cafés, Italian-speaking residents, and a plethora of trattorias. Sit in a café, buy an espresso or cappuccino, and listen to the Italian conversation swirling around you. You may not understand all the gossip, but you will certainly enjoy the animated chatter. The sense of community is palpable; close-knit families are the norm. One young restaurateur who grew up here recalls in *Boston Magazine,* "You never went further than a couple of blocks—or where you could hear your mother yelling and she could hear you. Besides, everybody knew everybody, so if you got in trouble on one street, your father would have heard about it already by the time you were able to run home."

However, the North End has not always been an Italian neighborhood; its history is very American—the Old North Church, the Paul Revere House, and Copp's Hill Burying Ground are all here. The area has hosted successive waves of immigrants, beginning with the Puritans in 1630. The Tories made this an upscale neighborhood until they fled on the eve of the Revolution. They were replaced by working-class colonists employed in the shipping trade. Seventy-five years later, poverty-stricken European immigrants—Irish, Eastern European Jews, and finally Italians—changed the face and sounds of the neighborhood. Dozens of families crammed into existing houses, and tenements were born; conditions were appalling. Circumstances like these encouraged the rise of ethnic politicians. Over 100 years ago, renowned John F. "Honey Fitz" Fitzgerald, grandfather to President John F. Kennedy, served as United States congressman and the city's first Catholic mayor. He was a "dearo," not a dear old man, but a "dear old North Ender" who paved the way for James Michael Curley and the many Irish politicians who followed him. Although Eastern European Jews also lived here, they were not dearos—they were merchants of clothing, dry goods, housewares, and groceries. On Hanover Street two 20th-century retail giants got their start in pushcarts. First on the block was Eben Marsh, followed by Rowland H. Macy. After 145 years of friendly competition, Macy's finally bought out Jordan Marsh.

Nor were the Italians "dearos," but they became the *true* dear old North Enders. Although they comprised only one third of the population in the 1860s, they stayed and started buying real estate. As the Irish and the Jews left for the suburbs, the Italians changed the face of the community, creating a homogeneous area, which, by 1935, was 95 percent Italian. Yet within this community subtle distinctions existed. Villages emigrated together, creating enclaves both regional and occupational: fishermen from the southern coast and Sicily lived near the waterfront; bakers and butchers from the interior lived closer to the shopping district. Small-town life successfully crossed the Atlantic. Old-timers interviewed by *Boston Magazine* recall "a time when pushcart vendors strolled the streets and women did their shopping by lowering baskets from windows to the street so vendors could fill them with vegetables, bread or meats. Everything was transacted on the honor system—accounts were settled at the end of the month."

Even in this urban area, vegetables and flowers sprouted from rooftop gardens, and winemaking was an annual event. Relief from tenement life was found in the omnipresent men's clubs and, in warm weather, on the sidewalk. In summer, people spilled out onto the street, and the whole neighborhood became a communal living room.

Festivals honoring saints were (and still are) the great occasions of the summer season, with their gala parades, dancing, and booths of foodstuffs and souvenirs. The August Fisherman's Feast, organized by the Madonna Del Soccorso Di Sciacca Society, is still extravagant. The festivities begin with a parade in which the Madonna is carried through the streets, accompanied by a lively brass band. People welcome her by vying to pin dollars onto her train; others greet her enthusiastically from their open windows. Suspended by a pulley, a young girl masquerading as an angel soars over the crowd. The release of white doves makes a spectacular finale. But the celebration continues: music, crooned by middle-aged would-be Dean Martins, floats through the night from a stage bedecked with hundreds of lightbulbs.

Though the *festes* have become more commercial, they represent the character and the charm of the Italian North End. Still, a tremendous demographic shift has occurred. That a Starbucks can survive on the edge of espresso-land is an indication of the trend toward yuppification. *The Boston Globe* recently detailed statistics that reveal the changes transforming one North End block. In 1930 there were 42 adults and 60 children; the average monthly rent was $28; wives did not work; men were fishermen and laborers; most couples had at least three children. Today, there are 57 people on the block—all adults; rent for a two-bedroom apartment is at least $1,500; there are no fishermen. The residents are white single professionals with few, if any, Italian genes. Another way of looking at this same phenomenon was articulated by a resident: "When I was a kid, there were a hundred butchers and five restaurants; today there are five butchers and a hundred restaurants." Some bemoan the influx of newcomers; others realize the neighborhood is strong enough to absorb them and maintain its old-fashioned virtues. As visitors' ears are charmed by the sound of the Italian language, their noses are tantalized by the aroma of garlic, sage, and freshly baked breads. City Councilor Paul Scapicchio observed, "The yuppies love to cook Italian food. When they move to the North End, they all become a little Italian."

At the time of his move to this house, Paul Revere was becoming increasingly involved in the fight for American self-determination. His work with the Continental Congress, his arduous freedom rides to New Hampshire, New York, and Philadelphia, and his contributions to the events leading up to the Revolutionary War have earned him a place in history as a true Son of Liberty. Although his name is associated with the opening days of the Revolution, he was not considered a hero in his time.

He lived in this building, now called the **Paul Revere House [24],** during the crucial decade of 1770–80. Shortly after the death of his first wife, he followed the custom of the day, remarrying five months later. This practice was rooted in necessity; two parents were needed to care for the large families that were the norm. Revere already had eight children when he became a widower, and with his second wife, fathered eight more. However, with a span of 30 years between the oldest and the youngest, there were never more than eight living here at the same time. And Revere worked hard to support his brood. A talented metalworker, he crafted beautiful silver tea sets (on display at the Museum of Fine Arts—see Indoor Foot Notes), copper engravings, church bells, and even dental wiring. At the age of 66 he became a true entrepreneur, opening a copper

‼️
Turn right onto Richmond Street; turn left onto North Street to Paul Revere House

mill in nearby Canton and covering Boston from top to bottom; he rolled out sheets of copper for the dome of the State House and the hull of the battleship known as "Old Ironsides."

The house was already 90 years old when Revere bought it. Its sharply pitched roof, casement windows and overhanging second story are medieval in style; an American interpretation of 16th-century Elizabethan architecture. It was designed to protect the family from the harsh New England winter: windows are small and shuttered, ceilings are low, huge fireplaces dominate each room. There are no halls—it would have been a waste of fuel to heat them.

This building and its red-brick neighbor, the **Pierce-Hichborn House [24],** survived as the neighborhood deteriorated because subsequent owners converted them to tenements with storefronts. The Revere House itself morphed from candy store to cigar factory to Jewish produce market to Italian bank. In 1907 it was restored by Revere descendants and looks very much as it did originally (without the third floor added by Revere for his children). The short tour of the house is highly recommended for the rare and accurate glimpse it gives of colonial life. There is little that actually belonged to the Reveres here, but the furnishings are all typical of the period.

It is interesting to note that although the distinguished Pierce-Hichborn House was built only 30 years after the Revere House it represents another architectural vocabulary. This early-18th-century residence was constructed of brick

Note red-brick house to left of Revere House

in response to the destructive fires that frequently cut a swath through Boston in its early years. It is far more sophisticated in style than its unpretentious neighbor.

Revere House looks out on North Square

North Square's [25] underwhelming cobblestone triangle, with its imposing chain, acknowledges the square's nautical past. The adjacent Sacred Heart Catholic Church is the former home of mid-19th-century Methodist preacher Father Edward Taylor. His charismatic sermons were directed at sailors but also attracted visitors such as Whitman, Emerson, and Dickens. Emerson called him "the Shakespeare of the sailor and the poor." He built the Mariner's House on the left side of the square, where seamen still board. In Taylor's day the square was not filled with tourist buses but rather "brothels, rat pits, dance halls, gambling joints and saloons." Sailors were lured here, seduced by the temptations of the neighborhood; fortunately, they were able to repent on Sunday mornings in Taylor's church. One hundred and fifty years earlier, the local preachers were not as forgiving. Although their church no longer exists, the Mather family, three generations of powerful Puritan clergy—Increase, Cotton, and Samuel—preached their stern gospel here.

Continue on North Street; make left onto Prince Street; turn right onto Hanover Street; continue for two blocks

The doctrine preached from the pulpit of **Saint Stephen's Church [26]** has changed three times: from Congregational to Unitarian to Catholic, reflecting neighborhood demographics. It was also repositioned, literally, to adapt to neighborhood needs: first it was moved back 12 feet to accommodate the widening of Hanover Street;

then it was raised to make room for a basement chapel. Shabby and deteriorating by 1964, it was put back in its original position and refurbished by Richard Cardinal Cushing. The building stands today as it looked when it was rehabbed by Charles Bulfinch in 1804 (see Beacon Hill Walk). It is the only remaining church of the five he designed in Boston—a fine example of his work's eloquent simplicity and balance. The Italianate tower that differentiates Saint Stephen's from other classical Federal-style churches indicates his architectural creativity.

As if Bulfinch were prescient, his campanile faces the typically Italian urban park, known as the **Prado [27],** which was created in 1933. The *AIA Guide to Boston* notes, "Certainly the Mall's designer, Arthur Shurtleff, had in the back of his mind the wonderful spatial sequences of Venice and other Italian cities when he conceived this." Earlier in the 20th century, this shady refuge, where children now play and old folks gather, rivaled Calcutta for population density. Mayor James Michael Curley, in one of his urban improvement projects, razed the slums and mandated this as community space, officially the **Paul Revere Mall [27].** Its centerpiece statue, sculpted by Cyrus Dallin in 1885 and cast in 1940, evokes different emotions among critics. While some consider it a masterpiece of strength and determination, others find it pretentious—doubting whether Revere would even recognize himself.

What would he have thought of his portrayal in Longfellow's patriotic poem "Paul Revere's Ride"? This poem, memorized by thousands of

Cross Hanover Street; stroll through the Prado (Paul Revere Mall)

Proceed to Old North Church at top of steps at far end of Paul Revere Mall

American schoolchildren, does not tell the whole story. But the **Old North Church [28],** cited by Longfellow, did play a leading role in the historic events of April 18, 1775. The colonists, watchful for British troop movement, had devised a plan to send riders across the countryside to warn of attack. As a contingency plan, Revere had arranged with Robert Newman, the sexton of Old North, to signal with lanterns from the belfry, "one if by land, and two if by sea." It was a precaution in case Paul Revere and his co-riders were captured—a way of identifying the British route to the patriots across the Charles River.

On the night the soldiers began to mobilize, Revere furtively rowed across the river to Charlestown just under the 64 guns of the HMS *Somerset.* The sound of his oars was muffled by a flannel petticoat thrown to him by a young patriot. On the other side, he was given a horse and galloped west. Right behind him, the regulars, crack British troops, were heading west as well. Their goals were to capture John Hancock and Sam Adams, who were hiding in Lexington, and to destroy munitions stored in Concord.

At the same time, without awakening the soldiers quartered in his house, Newman crept past the regulars patrolling the street, dashed up to the bell tower of Old North, flashed two lights across the river, climbed out of the church window, and stealthily returned home over the rooftops.

Although it was Revere whom Longfellow chose to celebrate, 35 other men rode from town to town—their names were just not as mellifluous. In fact, Revere never did make it as far as Concord: he was captured by British soldiers, who took his horse but miraculously let him go. Most famous of the fellow riders were William Dawes (see Cambridge Walk) and Dr. Samuel Prescott. Only Prescott, a local familiar with the countryside, successfully made it all the way to Concord. But the

Interior of
Old North Church

alarm was sounded, and the minutemen beat back the regulars on the morning of April 19, 1775, when "the shot heard round the world" began the American Revolution. Interestingly, for many years, Revere was not even mentioned in history books. Longfellow glorified him in order to inspire Northerners to take up arms in the Civil War.

New Englanders are proud of this history and on Patriot's Day reenact the events of April 18 and 19, even hanging two lanterns in the belfry of the Old North Church. Though its official name is Christ Church, it is known to all as Old North and looks very much as it did almost 290 years ago. Its architect, William Price, not formally trained, was actually a draftsman and print dealer. Obviously a natural talent, he based his 1723 design on those of English architect Christopher Wren. The interior is simple and serene. It literally shimmers with light. However, critic Donlyn Lyndon credits the "mellow glow" to the site rather than the architect: "Courtyards surrounding the building capture the sunlight, filter it through trees and reflect modified light into the space of the church."

A 10-minute guided tour of the interior is recommended. If none is offered during your visit, walk through on your own past the high-sided pews, which were built this way to keep parishioners warm. Pew owners decorated them individually with cushions, upholstery, and foot heaters. The Revere family pew is #54. Note the graceful wineglass pulpit and elegant brass chandeliers dating from 1724. If the trumpeting cherubim on the back balcony seem a bit fanciful for this early American–style space, it is because these Belgian Baroque angels were most likely intended for a French church in Quebec. Parishioner Thomas Gruchy, a privateer, presented them as a gift to the church in 1746—booty from a captured French ship en route to Canada. Also noteworthy is the bust of George Washington that stands in the far left corner, modeled after a 1790 sculpture by Christian Cullager. General Lafayette said that it resembled the great man more than any other likeness. The window in the far right corner is the very one through which Robert Newman made his surreptitious escape.

Parishioner John Child's leaps from the Old North were not as secretive. Contemporary reports disclose that in 1757 he "flew" from the top of the steeple on three different occasions and lived to tell the tale. Some pictures show him outfitted with wings modeled after the drawings of Leonardo da Vinci; another story has him descending under a canopy-shaped contrivance. He got only three tries, however, because the town fathers ordered him to stop "since the spectacle caused people to take off from their labors."

It does not take a leap of faith to picture this magnificent steeple towering over the 18th-century landscape. Although the full stature of Old North is somewhat dwarfed by adjacent buildings, it seems proportionally and historically in tune with its setting. Unlike the Old South Meeting House and the Old State House, it is not hemmed in by giant skyscrapers; the brick buildings of the North End rarely stand more than five stories high.

Walk up Hull Street across from Old North Church; enter Copp's Hill on your right

The magnificently sited **Copp's Hill [29]** is the final resting place for this walk. Named for a 17th-century English farmer, this graveyard is similar to others along the walk. What is extraordinary here is the location. From this vantage point one can see history unfold. Charlestown, to which Paul Revere rowed to get a horse, is ahead of you. The Bunker Hill Monument and "Old Ironsides" (see Waterfront and Charlestown Walk) are visible when the trees are not in leaf. And the gravestone of Captain Daniel Malcolm indicates both the proximity and the reality of the history that shaped this nation 235 years ago. The headstone is marred with bullet holes—the British used it for target practice, possibly incited by the inscription:

Proceed to Malcolm's gravestone on left side of cemetery, near the central path

> *A true Son of Liberty, a Friend to the*
> *Publick, An Enemy to Oppression and*
> *One of the foremost in opposing the*
> *Revenue Acts on America*

Also known as Corpse Hill, the setting accommodated, astoundingly, more than 10,000 burials. The headstones are engraved with the now-familiar Puritan symbols of death: skeletons, skulls, and hourglasses. Imagine the reaction of patrons of a local bakery when they discovered baked into the bottom of their bread these Puritan funereal symbols. It was not the hand of the devil but the work of thieves who stole headstones to meet the needs of the living—from building houses to constructing ovens. Oh, if these stones could talk! This hill has been witness to the serene, the hostile, and the incredible.

Overlooking tranquil Boston Harbor, one might envision a picturesque roiling sea with large waves breaking along the shore. But the concept of a 30-foot wave of molasses seems beyond the imagination. Yet just such a rogue wave thundered in on January 15, 1919, when 2 million gallons of hot molasses broke through a storage tank and burst onto **Commercial Street.** The viscous liquid was propelled with such force and speed that everything in its path was destroyed—houses, the elevated railway, railcars, and people. Twenty-one died and over 150 were injured. The cause of the flood is not known, though some surmise that unusually warm winter weather caused the molasses to expand; it is more likely that the tank was structurally defective. The owner, U.S. Industrial Alcohol, paid out over $1 million in damages. The molasses was not bound for kitchens and bakeries; instead, the "military industrial complex" had created a huge demand for alcohol distilled from the sticky syrup for its munitions factories. Recent research suggests that the tank was placed in dangerous proximity to a densely populated neighborhood because the poor immigrants who lived here had no means of protest. It took over a week to clean up the congealed muck—it was finally cleared away by hosing down the area with seawater. Is it just an olfactory memory, or as some old-timers maintain, can you still smell molasses here on unusually warm days?

A bit of lost Boston tradition stands across Hull Street—a house that is known as a "ten-footer."

Commercial Street lies between Copp's Hill and Boston Harbor

Return to Hull Street

Number 44 [30] is a rare remaining example. Barely 9 feet, 6 inches wide, it is the slimmest house in Boston. Built circa 1800, it resembles other humble abodes shown in illustrations of colonial architecture. But its legend has made it a celebrity: known as "the spite house," it was supposedly built to block the light and view of the house behind it. Now, hardly spiteful, it is a charming reminder of the past and easy to miss, overshadowed by multiplex neighbors.

❗❗
Walk back down Hull Street; walk right on Salem Street

❗❗
When leaving the North End, walk back on Hanover Street to Haymarket T station at corner of New Sudbury and Congress Streets

Salem Street, more than the well-touristed Hanover Street, has the ambience of a small European city. Narrow, with a thin strip of sky above, it is lined with butcher, bread, and grocery stores. Here North Enders make their daily rounds. On sunny days, women sit on their stoops and catch up on local gossip much as they did 100 years ago. You too can share the spirit— shopping, eating, and meandering your way back to Hanover Street and Government Center. *Divertiteri*—enjoy!

Waterfront
and
Charlestown

"Huzza! Her sides are made of iron."
—Anonymous sailor

Essential Information for Walk Five

Length of walk:	2 ⅓ miles
Terrain:	flat with 2 short hills
Time:	2 ½ hours at a leisurely pace, without going inside any of the buildings
Nearest T stop:	South Station on Red Line
Starting point:	Exit T and cross Summer Street. Keeping Federal Reserve Building on your right, walk 2 blocks on Atlantic Avenue to Pearl Street. Cross to Greenway and stand in front of InterContinental Hotel.

Supplements to the Walk

Highly Recommended

Quick visit to Warren Tavern

Time:	5 minutes
Hours:	weekdays from 11:15 A.M.–10:30 P.M.; weekends from 10:30 A.M.
Telephone:	617-241-8142
Admission:	free
When:	second third of walk at 2 Pleasant Street

Battle of Bunker Hill Museum

Time:	30 minutes
Hours:	daily, 9:00 A.M.–5:00 P.M.
Telephone:	617-242-7275
Admission:	free
When:	last third of walk at 43 Monument Square

Tour of USS *Constitution*

Time:	20–30 minutes
Hours:	Apr.–Oct., Tues.–Sun., 10:00 A.M.–5:30 P.M., on the half-hour (last tour at 4:30 P.M.); Nov.– Mar., Thurs.–Sun., 10:00 A.M.–3:50 P.M., on the half-hour (last tour at 3:30 P.M.)
Telephone:	617-242-5671
Admission:	free
When:	last third of walk

HarborWalk

Time:	25–50 minutes
Hours:	at your discretion
When:	at end of walk

Of Further Interest

USS *Cassin Young*

Time:	45 minutes
Hours:	daily in summer, 10:00 A.M.–5:00 P.M.; tours at 11:00 A.M. and 2:00 P.M.; daily in winter, 12:00–3:00 P.M.
Telephone:	617-242-5601
Admission:	free
When:	last third of walk

Constitution **Museum**

Time:	25–60 minutes
Hours:	daily, Apr.–Oct., 9:00 A.M.–6:00 P.M.; daily, Nov.–Mar. 10:00 A.M.–5:00 P.M.
Telephone:	617-242-1812
Admission:	free; donation suggested
When:	last third of walk

Waterfront

Waterfront and Charlestown - Walk Five

Waterfront

1. InterContinental Hotel
2. Rowe's Wharf
3. Mother's Walk
4. *The Harbor Fog*
5. Rings Fountain
6. Christopher Columbus Park

Navy Yard and Charlestown

Navy Yard

7. Muster House
8. Commandant's House
9. USS *Constitution*

Charlestown

10. View of Zakim Bridge
11. Winthrop Square
12. #16 Common Street
13. #5 Common Street
14. Bunker Hill Monument
15. Charlestown High School
16. Warren Tavern
17. #119 Main Street
18. Austin Block
19. #55 Main Street— Deacon Larkin House
20. Battle of Bunker Hill Museum

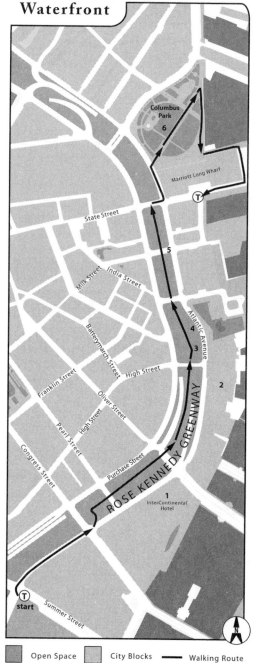

Open Space   City Blocks   ━ Walking Route

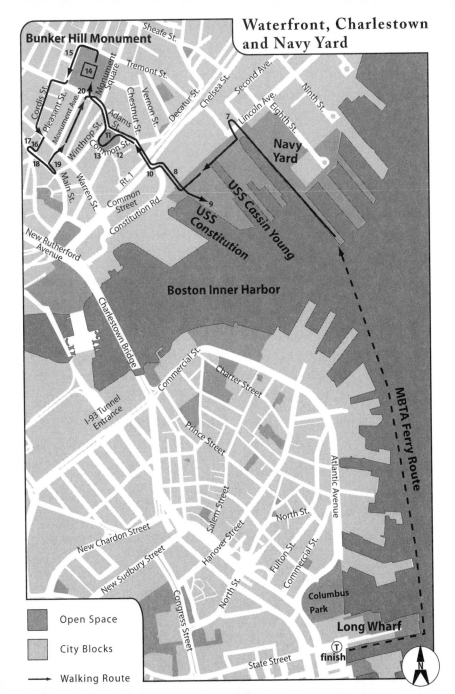

Waterfront, Charlestown and Navy Yard

Sheafe St.

Bunker Hill Monument

15

14

Tremont St.

Monument Square

20

Monument Ave.

Cordis St.

Pleasant St.

17 16

18 19

Winthrop St.

Common St.

Adams St.

Chestnut St.

Vernon St.

Decatur St.

Chelsea St.

Second Ave.

Lincoln Ave.

Eighth St.

Ninth St.

7

Navy Yard

11

13 12

Rt. 1

10 8

9

USS Cassin Young

USS Constitution

Main St.

Warren St.

Common Street

Constitution Rd.

New Rutherford Avenue

Charlestown Bridge

Boston Inner Harbor

I-93 Tunnel Entrance

Commercial St.

Charter Street

Prince Street

Salem Street

Hanover Street

North St.

Atlantic Avenue

MBTA Ferry Route

New Chardon Street

New Sudbury Street

Congress Street

North St.

Fulton St.

Commercial St.

Columbus Park

Long Wharf

State Street

T finish

Open Space

City Blocks

Walking Route

N

Build it and they shall come . . .

Boston's "field of dreams" can now be found at the **Rose Kennedy Greenway,** opening the soul of Boston—its waterfront—to the rest of the city. Hear the voices of locals discovering Boston's new outdoor space:

You sit on the grass and decide you might want to play hooky every afternoon, amazed that something this good eventually came out of the Big Dig.

This is one of my favorite places in Boston. Dry up about the lack of typical parkiness (i.e., grass and trees). This is downtown Boston!

Whoever first proposed the idea of the Greenway must have received the same quizzical looks that Walt Disney received upon suggesting the idea of Disneyland: "You want to do what with Route I-93? Put it underground and put a park on top? Right . . ."

How romantical!

This expanse of green is a delight for anybody, but for Bostonians, who suffered through 16 years of construction, it is a celebration. As we braved the detours and traffic jams caused by the never-ending $14 billion Big Dig, we smiled cynically at a waggish billboard that proclaimed, "Rome wasn't built in a day—if it was we would have hired their contractor."

Imagine standing under a hulking elevated highway, all your senses being bombarded: thundering traffic overhead, acrid exhaust fumes, obstructed field of vision. You couldn't hear yourself think; you couldn't converse; and you certainly couldn't enjoy the view. All of these problems have been buried, along with the highway.

The Greenway, a 15-acre, 1.5-mile-long meandering ribbon of open space, is the result of visionary public and private groups, which, in 2004, united to form the nonprofit Rose Fitzgerald Kennedy Greenway Conservancy, the official steward of the area. The long-awaited opening ceremony took place in October 2008 with much fanfare and revelry. Attending luminaries included many Kennedy family members as well as New York City's Mayor Michael Bloomberg, who grew up here. Concerned about the possibility of encroaching real estate, Boston's Mayor Tom Menino promised to start work immediately on zoning restrictions, ensuring that tall buildings would never overshadow the Greenway. And there are three additions on the drawing board—two museums and an outdoor food market.

Running south to north, the Greenway is divided into four sections—Chinatown, Dewey Square, the Wharf, and North End—each designed to reflect the spirit and architecture of its surrounding neighborhood. The two middle sections (where you will walk) merge with the waterfront and pay homage to the sea. The straight path on the western edge of the Greenway mimics the facing buildings' rigid façades; the interior walkways are more fluid, undulating like the inner harbor.

Because of the mass of the **InterContinental Hotel [1],** one might not realize that its 22-story towers are the same height as the masts of the tall ships that originally anchored here; their bowed shape is analogous to billowing sails. In describing the color of the building, architect Howard Elkus says, "It is not a blue building, but sometimes it's very blue; sometimes it's all about clouds. What it's about is motion . . . The curved glass façade reflects the light and the sky throughout the day and night and through the year." The color varies from blue to gray, as does the sea, both taking their hues and clues from above.

‼

Keeping InterContinental on your right, walk north, crossing Oliver Street

The hues and clues of the plantings here are taken from the Massachusetts Horticultural Society, whose creativity and painterly approach are richly on display. The permanent "collection" is complemented with changing containers and seasonal plantings. A stroll through the tall grasses offers a few moments of tranquility amidst the urban landscape.

Mass Hort, one of Boston's most illustrious institutions, claims to have "invented" the Concord grape, the Bartlett pear, and the landscaped cemetery. At one time, the society conferred such respectability that, upon proffering their membership cards, women were automatically granted department store credit cards. Today Mass Hort has lost its green pockets but not its green thumb.

On your right, at High Street, is the splendid Boston Harbor Hotel, part of the **Rowe's Wharf [2]** complex completed in 1987. A staple of the waterfront much before the recent changes, it has always related to the grandeur and strength of Boston's nautical heritage. Rowe's Wharf is a superb fusion of public and private space, of city and waterfront, and of horizontal and vertical. Here stands a luxury hotel, part of a development, the architecture of which responds to both the office buildings of the financial district and the piers of the harbor. These figurative connections are made practical by a waterside walkway and docks for commuter boats from the airport and coastline suburbs. The dramatic metaphor for this rapport between the city and the sea is the grand archway, which is both a symbolic welcome and an architectural coup de théâtre.

Keep walking north on Greenway

The immensity of the Rowe's Wharf structure is oddly balanced by the simplicity of the **Mother's Walk [3]** paving stones at your feet. One could easily miss them. Don't. As this park honors one of Boston's most revered mothers, so these six-inch-square pavers pay tribute to less known, but equally cherished mothers and caregivers. A $500 contribution to the Greenway enables anyone to simultaneously honor a loved one and support this project.

On your right, between High and India Streets, is a series of textured constructions, a nautical composition by Ross Miller entitled *The Harbor Fog* **[4]**. His artistic concern was to realize the connection between the site and the composition, thus enhancing the experience of being in a very specific place. Move around the installation: it exhales the heavy mist that can envelop this harbor area for days. Motion detectors trigger the sounds of warning foghorns, while pulsating LED lights, reminiscent of harbor buoys, signal caution. The surrounding granite boulders are salvaged from sea walls. One is so large it might allude to the hidden dangers faced by 19th-century schooners. Unlike many urban parks, the Greenway is open after dark, and this scene is dazzling at night.

The next section of the Greenway, between India and State Streets, is called the **Great Room.** Twelve tall structures bookmark and illuminate this area, which is flat and open to accommodate outdoor performances. As with the towers of the InterContinental Hotel, these theatrical fixtures can be interpreted as sails of a clipper ship. The highlight of this "room" is the **Rings Fountain [5],** which puts on its own show during the summer months. Watching the playful geysers can be an addictive pastime. Children enjoy the challenge of running through the unpredictable choreography of these waterspouts that soak them if they get the timing wrong . . . or right.

This is an ideal spot to admire the iconic **Custom House.** Its unique clock tower looms on the left behind 20th-century office buildings and 19th-century wharf warehouses. A charming relic of Boston's nautical history (see Downtown and North End Walk), it is the perfect vantage point from which to gauge how much land was reclaimed from the sea to create this neighborhood: the ocean once lapped at its doorstep.

The arbors of **Christopher Columbus Park [6]** are alluring in all seasons. Adorned in blue wiste-

👣

At State Street, cross Atlantic Avenue; walk 1 1/2 blocks north to Christopher Columbus Park. Walk through first two arbors

ria in late spring, the foliage provides a luxuriant respite from the summer heat. Draped in blue fairy lights in the winter, they become a sparkling backdrop to the annual Presidents' Day ice-carving contest. The softness of the wisteria and the magic of the lights marvelously frame Commercial Wharf straight ahead, which is now less a site of commerce than of many great "rooms with a view."

Finally, **Boston Harbor!** Just glimpsed through the arch at Rowe's Wharf, and referenced throughout the Greenway, this waterfront vista marries the old and the new, the land and the sea, enterprise and romance. And Senator Teddy Kennedy saw even more, quipping, "On a clear day you can see all the way to Ireland." The scene unfolds in the upcoming 10-minute ferry ride.

From its inception Boston's fortunes have been married inescapably to the sea. A romantic interlude in this long seafaring history is the age of the glamorous clipper ships. . . . It was the 1840s. The California Gold Rush was inspiring potential prospectors all across America. People pinned their hopes on possible gold and set their hearts on speed; out of this marriage of desire, greed, and need was born the clipper ship. Every element of her design was subsumed in the name of speed . . . [the] profusion of sails—on masts often as high as twenty-story buildings—was their only seeming ostentation, but it was a necessary one; ships usually sailed with each one unfurled to harness every scrap of wind, often taking the breath of those watching from shore. The term "clipper" was derived from the word "clip," as in "to go at a good

Walk down stairs on right to esplanade. Continue along waterside, walking around back of Marriott Hotel to Charlestown ferry (T stop) on left

We suggest reading pages 197–202 of the text while waiting to board the ferry. You will then be able to enjoy the view from the outside deck. Board ferry

Ferry leaving
Long Wharf

clip." Some logged more than 400 miles a day . . .
Many set sailing records that would remain un-
broken for over 100 years.

Historian John Harris dramatically conveys a picture of maritime Boston in the mid-19th century.
The sleek pleasure yachts anchored here today are
the descendants of the clippers, adorning the current scene with their graceful silhouettes. The
freighters that still carry on the hard work of
trade are docked beyond your view.

This harbor has been bustling for the past 300
years. By 1722 Boston boasted more than three
dozen wharves, more than a dozen shipyards,
and a half-dozen ropewalks—testimony to the

importance of the sea trade to this town of 12,000 inhabitants. In the 19th century, as trade came in, Boston "wharfed out"; the buildings seemed to step forth to meet the cargo. The entrepreneurs who fostered the wharf expansion included Harrison Gray Otis, Francis C. Lowell, and Charles Bulfinch (names familiar from other walks). Those who did business here included Boston's First Families: the Higginsons, the Amorys, and the Perkinses. Their merchandise came from all over the world—Asian porcelain, French millinery, Indian silk, as well as Caribbean sugar and molasses. The ships also transported human cargo—terrified Africans destined to be slaves as well as hopeful immigrants from Ireland, Italy, and Eastern Europe. Harris continues: "The romantic age of the clipper ship was short-lived, as many ardent romances are. With the end of the Civil War, the Depression of 1857, and the rise of the railroad and other steam-propelled travel, clipper trade virtually disappeared." And with it disappeared the affluence that had marked this era.

It wasn't until the mid-20th century that Boston Harbor was revitalized. The warehouses that survived were converted into trendy condominiums and offices. Hotels, restaurants, parks, and shops have proliferated, and as they have flourished, the vitality has become palpable. As the ferry pulls away from **Long Wharf,** note the grouping of the 1982 **Long Wharf Marriott Hotel,** the 1763 **Chart House,** and the 1845 **Custom House Block,** an altogether satisfying historical and architectural amalgam with a unifying nautical theme. The Marriott, with its vaguely shiplike profile and substantial mass, was designed to relate to its more indigenous neighbors. The Chart House is the only remaining prerevolutionary structure of the many that had lined the wharf. John Hancock had his office here, and his safe still remains on the second floor. The Custom House Block is uniquely interesting: from the front it appears to be a functional assemblage of granite warehouses, whereas the back, faced with red brick, has a completely different personality—warmer and less imposing.

Long Wharf, built in 1710, is appropriately named. During the 19th century the wharf kept growing, eventually reaching a length of more than 1,800 feet. Its extension into the deeper waters of the harbor allowed even the largest ships to unload their cargo safely. At the time of the wharf's construction, Boston was the busiest port in the colonies; by 1850, over 1,000 ships traded here. With its warehouses, counting houses, customs houses, and shops, it was not only the shipping center of the town, but the portal through which everything and everyone passed. Long Wharf was the landmark that symbolized Boston, much as the Eiffel Tower signifies Paris.

There were many reasons for passing through Long Wharf. John Singleton Copley, the 18th-century painter-to-be, played here outside his mother's tobacco shop. The redcoats, who could not decide if they were coming or going, did both, until they were successfully driven out in 1776. In 1819, the first missionaries to Hawaii sailed off to convert the heathen. And 1895 was the year that Joshua Slocum embarked on the first around-the-world solo voyage, an endeavor that would take more than three years. While most people romanticized the seafaring life, in the 1840s a young customs inspector who worked here expressed his contempt for it: "Long Wharf is devoted to ponderous, evil-smelling, inelegant necessities of life." This disenchanted bureaucrat was Nathaniel Hawthorne, who fortuitously found another career.

Commercial Wharf was considered the most exclusive of these "outcroppings" because it specialized in foreign trade. According to a contemporary chronicler, déclassé lobster and fishing boats were not welcome at this upscale pier. That notwithstanding, it was the home port for the commonplace ice that was cut in New England and shipped to warmer climes. When Frederic Tudor first began shipping ice blocks in 1806, people laughed. Within 25 years, this strange concept had boosted the economy of the small towns fortunate enough to capitalize on their frozen assets.

The adjacent wharves have been beautifully rehabbed and gentrified. On lovely spring days, it is hard not to covet their easy access to the waterfront; yet Boston winters make life harsh even in this idyllic setting. It is on these blustery, cold, dreary days that one can imagine these wharves as home to some shadowy activities in the 19th century. The little brick **Pilot House,** built by the Union Railroad in the 1860s, was innocently used as a rendezvous for train engineers and ship pilots. Yet, when a false floor was removed in 1972, it seemed likely to investigators that this space

Once the ferry is under way, the wharves can be seen off to the left

cached contraband, probably opium. And at **Lewis Wharf,** next door, a more sinister discovery was made. During a reconstruction in 1800, two skeletons were found in a secret underground tunnel—locked in their final embrace. Rumor has it that the skeletal remains were those of the young wife of an elderly man and her sailor lover, caught by the avenging husband.

Step even further back from today's bustling port scene and imagine how this spot looked to the Puritans almost 400 years ago. In 1629, approaching the land that would become Charlestown, they anticipated:

> *The Kingly Lyon, and the strong arm'd Beare.*
> *The large lim'd Mooses, with the tripping Deere.*
> *Quill darking Porcupines and Rackoones be*
> *Castell'd in the hollow of an Aged tree.*
> —New England Prospects

There had been reports of a plentitude of cod, clams, herring, and lobster. But alas, these rumors were propaganda for emigration. Dismayed with their first stop in inhospitable Salem, the Puritans moved on to this promising harbor, but it yielded neither abundant food nor potable water. Many of the original group died within the first year. After a second disastrous winter in Charlestown, future governor John Winthrop led his flock across the Charles River to what is now Boston (see Downtown and North End Walk). A feisty few remained, ultimately taming the wilderness and creating a viable settlement, including a church, a school, a mill, and, by 1641, the settlement's first shipyard.

This maritime tradition continues to be celebrated today at the **Charlestown Navy Yard,** a
part of the Boston National Historic Park. Commissioned in 1800 by President John Adams, the
yard's first assignment was the 74-gun *Independence,* completed during the War of 1812. The facility's primary function, however, was not
shipbuilding but naval maintenance and repair.
Another mandate was supplying the sailors with
"slops," not navy food, but a 19th-century catchall
word for military clothing and sundries.

❗❗
Walk down dock
into Navy Yard

For more than 135 years all the rope used by the
U.S. Navy was made here at the quarter-mile-
long building called the Ropewalk. The method
of manufacturing rope necessitated a facility of
this extraordinary size: fibers were wrapped
around the workers' waists and as they walked the
length of the building the fibers were guided into
the spinning mechanism. The ropewalk became
obsolete in the 1970s when synthetic fibers replaced natural hemp. In this building, the presti-
gious architect Alexander Parris demonstrated
the credo "form follows function." The building
stands empty at the back of the property, a long,
low, drab gray rectangle, today a form without
function.

During the Civil War the pace of work acceler-
ated in the yard, but it wasn't until the 1930s,
with World War II looming, that shipbuilding
increased exponentially. A decade of frenetic pro-
ductivity was supported by more than 50,000 laborers: over 150 ships were launched—46 in 1943
alone. The work at the Charlestown Navy Yard
epitomized the huge war effort, and the town

thrived. But when World War II ended, so did the need for warships—the last was built in 1956, and operations shut down in 1974. The same year, in recognition of the yard's contribution to America's victory, Congress designated these 30 acres as a historic site. In addition to serving as a tribute to the U.S. Navy, this area has become a remarkable demonstration of land reclamation. New construction is complemented by rehabbed historic buildings now serving as research facilities, offices, and mixed-income housing.

Most of the yard's distinctive buildings were erected in the 19th century. The appealing octagonal brick building straight ahead is the **Muster House [7],** completed in 1854. Here nonmilitary employees reported to work and received their salaries; by 1890 it was functioning as the yard's first telephone exchange. Another outstanding building is the 1805 **Commandant's House [8].** Befitting the importance of such a senior officer, this elegant residence served as both his private home and the venue for official functions. Although the designer is unknown, many feel the style of the building suggests the influence of Charles Bulfinch (see Beacon Hill Walk), whose Federal period architecture is marked by balance and dignity. It is still a commanding property, today used for receptions and special events.

A variety of interesting sites here illuminate American history, but the **USS *Constitution* [9],** launched in 1797, is the heroine of this park. Her charmed life began with America's first victory at sea. Having won the Revolutionary War, the new country felt no immediate need for a navy, nor

Walk left, following brick path past *Constitution* Museum on left; look right just beyond tennis courts to Commandant's House

Walk to USS *Constitution* (three-masted schooner) on your left. (We suggest you tour the ship before taking return ferry.)

USS *Constitution*—
"Old Ironsides"

could it rally a force as formidable as Britain's fleet of 1,500 ships. However, the downside of independence was that the United States was no longer protected by British sea power, and, in the Mediterranean the Tripoli-based Barbary pirates were mercilessly attacking American merchant ships. At first, the United States paid protection money to the pasha of Tripoli; yet succumbing to bribery only made matters worse. By 1801 the demands for tribute became so exorbitant that a counterattack was launched under the slogan "Millions for defense, but not one cent for tribute." The newly built *Constitution* was one of six ships sent to thwart the buccaneers who were wreaking havoc with American trade. The virgin navy's successful foray into sea battle has been forever commemorated by the words of the United States Marine anthem: "From the halls of Montezuma to the shores of Tripoli . . ."

The USS *Constitution*'s record is extraordinary. She never lost a battle: she engaged in 42 conflicts and captured 20 vessels, and the only enemies who boarded her were prisoners of war. Though she never had to flee, her 36 sails would have enabled her to outrun any attacker. Her strongest offensive tactic was the ability of her guns to scatter a combination of glass and bone at the enemy's rigging, spraying opponents and rendering the barefoot sailors incapable of moving. Her most famous encounter was against the British frigate *Guerrière* in the War of 1812. During this conflict a sailor was heard to cry, "Huzza, her sides are made of iron," a technically incorrect but honest perception, for cannonballs appeared to bounce off the ship. The black-painted hull was not made of iron but of live oak, an especially strong wood from Georgia. The cannon fire was repelled, and the new nickname, "Old Ironsides," stuck.

Boston has been very loyal to this hometown ship, the oldest commissioned warship in the world still afloat. Remarkably, she survived three attempts at demolition. Her first savior was Oliver Wendell Holmes, who published an emotional, patriotic poem in *The Boston Daily Advertiser* in 1830. It would have been difficult to resist the sentimental entreaty of the last stanza:

Oh, better that her shattered bulk
Should sink beneath the wave;
Her thunders shook the mighty deep,
And there should be her grave;
Nail to the mast her holy flag,
Set every threadbare sail,
And give her to the god of storms.
The lightning and the gale!

In 1904, she was rescued by the Massachusetts Society of the Daughters of 1812; the navy had planned to use her for (*gasp!*) target practice. Finally in 1925, she was restored to her former glory by a fund-raising drive spearheaded by Boston's schoolchildren. Of the $250,000 raised, over half came from the children's penny donations. The *Constitution*'s farewell voyage in 1931 logged 22,000 miles of coastal America, bidding adieu at 90 ports. Today this venerable vessel sails into the harbor every Fourth of July for a cruise that is both nostalgic and practical. Upon her return, she reverses her anchorage so that both sides of the hull will weather evenly. This esteemed lady of the sea is toasted—and tooted—by all the boats in the harbor.

Return to narrowed red-brick path and follow it left; where the path forms a Y, bear right out of Navy Yard into Charlestown

The USS *Constitution* is one of Boston's historic stars; one of Boston's newest stars is the **Leonard P. Zakim Bunker Hill Bridge [10].** This magnificent structure is soaring and exuberant, yet utterly simple and effortless. Some have compared its inverted-Y-shaped towers to "a gigantic two-masted schooner sailing into the city's skyline." Others say the imagery of the towers reverberates with the historic symbol of Charlestown, their shape echoing the Bunker Hill Monument. As innovative in its fabrication as in its design, the bridge is the brainchild of Swiss engineer Christian Menn. Its cable-stayed construction is similar to that of a suspension bridge, but less costly. With the bridge accommodating ten lanes of traffic, Boston now boasts the largest bridge of this kind in the world.

Opened in 2003, the bridge became a *cause célèbre*. It was originally to be named for Lenny Zakim, the tireless director of Boston's Anti-Defamation League, who died at the age of 46. This inspired community leader worked toward uniting people of different faiths and races and has been recognized by cultural icons as disparate as Bruce Springsteen and Pope John Paul II. Yet

View of the
Zakim Bridge
from Charlestown

when Charlestown residents heard that the bridge was to be named for someone who had no affiliation with their neighborhood, they protested. Negotiation resulted in its unwieldy formal name, but since it has become the road more traveled, its working moniker has become the Zakim Bridge. Historian Thomas H. O'Connor characterizes the compromise as "linking the colonial traditions of Charlestown with the name of Lenny Zakim, a man who spent his life building bridges, uniting many of the communities that make up greater Boston."

The tunnel under the highway into the heart of Charlestown is a passage that represents the independence of this community from the rest of Boston. The two municipalities remained discrete until 1874, yet their histories are inextricably entwined. After all, they were both founded by the same hardy Puritans and sent their sons together to defend their ideals. **Winthrop Square [11],** laid out by the first settlers in the 1640s, was originally used as a common grazing area and militia parade ground, known as the Old Training Field. It was here that the young men of Charlestown learned to soldier—and from here that they marched off to the Battle of Bunker Hill in 1775, to the War of 1812; and to the Civil War. Those who did not return are honored by two war memorials. As you walk to the bottom of the square, pay special attention to **#16 Common Street [12],** the former Old Salem Turnpike Hotel, a popular coach stop in the 18th century. Also note **#5 Common Street [13],** a private brick home that once housed the Old Training Field School, a local version of West Point, built in 1827.

Turn left onto Adams Street; stop at corner of Adams and Common Streets; walk left to lower corner of Winthrop Square

‼️

Turn into park;
walk straight
ahead through
Revolutionary War
memorial; continue
toward Bunker Hill
Monument straight
ahead; turn left at
Monument Square;
climb stairs to
obelisk

Looming ahead of you is the famous **Bunker Hill Monument [14]**, a misnomer because it stands on Breed's Hill. But indeed, this is the site of the conflict historically known as the Battle of Bunker Hill. Here young American soldiers were empowered, learning that they could successfully fight against the eminently more experienced and better-equipped British. In fact, the colonists did not win this battle, but they lost far fewer men and far less pride than their opponents.

The complacent British had little respect for these unschooled farmers and volunteers whose most effective weapon was passion. An excerpt from a letter written by loyalist Ann Hulton illustrates the British perception:

> *In this [British] army are many of noble family, many very respectable, virtuous and amiable characters, and it grieves one that gentlemen, brave British soldiers, should fall by the hands of such despicable wretches as compose the banditti of the country; amongst whom there is not one that has the least pretension to be called a gentleman. They are a most rude, depraved, degenerate race, and it is a mortification to us that they speak English and can trace themselves from that stock.*

After their ignoble retreat from the Battles of Lexington and Concord in April 1775 (see Downtown and North End Walk) the British determined to control Boston by occupying the three highest points surrounding the harbor: Breed's Hill, Bunker Hill, and Dorchester Heights. Fortunately, their hubris led to procrastination. Conversely, the colonists, learning of the

Bunker Hill
Monument

British intent, quickly moved to take advantage
of their opponents' delay. On the evening of June
16, 1775, General Israel Putnam and Colonel
William Prescott led the colonial militia to defend this hill. By cover of night, they built tempo-
rary earthen fortifications called redoubts.
Although deployed to Bunker Hill, the troops
defended Breed's Hill. It is not clear to this day
whether they made a geographical mistake or a
strategic decision. At dawn, the British awoke,
mightily surprised that the rebels had thwarted
their plans. Arrogantly, wave after wave of redcoats marched up the hill in close formation,
straight into a barrage of fire from the colonists.

Over 1,000 of the 2,200 British troops were killed or wounded. The rebels' mantra, "Don't fire 'til you see the whites of their eyes," has been ascribed to Colonel Prescott, yet historians disagree about who, if anyone, issued this order. Leaders in other wars have been credited with the admonition, but the colonists' small reserves of ammunition certainly would have made this precaution appropriate.

Much information about the battle is ambiguous. It is still being studied, and 235 years later, new facts are coming to light. Even the number of defenders varies from 1,200 to as many as 4,000. But regardless of the number of patriots, in the end, when they were out of ammunition, they heroically fought the British bayonets with stones and rocks before retreating. The battle was over in two and a half hours.

Although the Puritan settlers were a rather homogeneous lot, recent research has confirmed that this early American army included at least three dozen men of color, and the likelihood of many more. An unsung hero was Salem Poor, a former slave, who had purchased his freedom and fought as a private. A petition signed by fourteen officers to the General Court of the Massachusetts Bay Colony attests to his participation in battle. He garnered more citations for bravery than any other soldier of the Revolution. The deeds performed by this "brave and gallant" soldier are not specified in the petition or elsewhere. It is only known that he survived this battle and continued to fight for the patriot cause.

The most eminent Bostonian to fall during the battle was Dr. Joseph Warren, a celebrated patriot who fought as a private despite his status as an officer. As head of the Revolutionary Committee on Safety, he sent Paul Revere on his famous ride; sadly, Revere identified Warren's body, recognizing the dental work that he had crafted. Abigail Adams wrote to her husband, John, "When he fell, liberty wept." The battle resulted in 450 rebel casualties, yet it was also responsible for the birth of American confidence, a turning point that united the colonists. News of the accomplishment spread quickly, and settlers from all the territories joined the fight.

Ironically, one of the captured cannons from Bunker Hill is enshrined in the Tower of London. According to author Paul Hogarth, "Some years ago . . . the old cannon was proudly shown to a visiting American. The American looked it over calmly; and then just as calmly said, 'Oh, I see, *you* have the cannon and *we* have the hill.' "

Like the battle it honors, this monument was constructed against tremendous odds. Fifty years after the Battle of Bunker Hill, Americans felt an affinity with ancient Greece and Rome, especially their democratic ideals and classical architecture. When the memorial column erected here in honor of Joseph Warren began to crumble, a group of local patriots organized to build a lasting tribute. An Egyptian-style obelisk was a typical commemorative symbol in ancient Rome, and hence, architect Solomon Willard designed the 221-foot structure in this style. This ambitious undertaking would require massive amounts of granite, which was plentiful in the Quincy quarries 12 miles away. But transporting these blocks of stone was a problem and its resolution spawned a new industry, the first commercial railroad. Horse-drawn railcars transferred the granite from the quarry to the harbor; ferries carried it across the river to Charlestown; it was then hauled up the hill. The process was tedious and extremely costly. Expenses grew faster than the monument, and when the money ran out, building was halted. It was feared that the obelisk would never be completed until the ladies stepped in to save the day—and the monument. Planning the ultimate bake sale, civic-minded editor and poet Sarah Josepha Hale brought together a group of determined Boston women. No half-baked affair, the sale netted an astonishing $30,035.53 after one week of fundraising. It is said that socialite Eliza Henderson Boardman Otis did her civic duty by selling kisses at $5 each. Though not a great beauty, she was the mayor's wife; could this have been the sweetest purchase?

The monument was finally dedicated in 1843. Its total cost of $134,000 would be the equivalent of $3 million today. It had been 18 years since the marquis de Lafayette, General Washington's great ally, had come from France to lay the cornerstone. He had been so moved by the occasion that he took home with him trunks full of Charlestown earth to be laid at his grave. The great orator Daniel Webster, who had delivered the ground-breaking speech, was on hand to deliver the dedication. According to historian Jane Holtz Kay, "the phrases [were] so in tune with the times that they 'fell in Doric beauty from the speaker's lips.' " His words reverberated with patriotic fervor as he spoke to the audience of 100,000, including President John Tyler and 13 veterans of the battle. The president's attendance was a tribute to this monument, the first erected through contributions from private citizens. Moreover, until the completion of the Washington Monument in 1885, the Bunker Hill Monument was the country's tallest and most famous tourist site.

As you leave the monument, be sure to notice the real **Bunker Hill.** The church spire emerging from behind the town roofs marks the unrealized battleground. At the time, there were no such landmarks, just a growing settlement protected by the surrounding undeveloped hills. The *Boston Globe*'s Brian MacQuarrie reports on recent research: "In Boston, history is always just below the surface. And in Charlestown, underneath a row of genteel gardens, in the middle of a teeming city, is believed to be a mass grave containing the bones of possibly dozens of British soldiers killed in one of the most important battles in American history." These gardens are on Concord Street, just off to your right as you walk around the Square. One local ironically notes, "No wonder our plants grow so well." This lovely residential area with its cultivated gardens hardly seems to have been the site of such a horrific battle, yet these recent findings underscore the tragedy of the war.

Despite routing the redcoats, after the Battle of Bunker Hill Charlestown experienced a pervasive

At far side of obelisk, look out over cityscape. Walk down rear steps to Monument Square; walk left along the perimeter

sense of loss and desolation. The British, flushed with Pyrrhic victory, ravaged the city, burning down more than 500 buildings. Although most of the residents fled for the duration of the war, they returned in 1781 and vigorously began to rebuild. Colonists who grew wealthy from Boston's sea trade built their mansions here and on the nearby slopes. Civil War shipbuilding created a need for more workers, many of whom settled downhill from their more upscale neighbors. Others were employed in local factories with national name recognition: Schrafft's Candy, the Diamond Match Company, Revere Sugar, and Hood Dairy. By the 20th century most of the population of Charlestown was Irish Catholic—a tightly knit, fiercely proud, working-class community. But as factories became more automated and the Navy Yard downsized, many lost their jobs. Buildings were converted to offices staffed by fewer employees, especially favoring those with white-collar credentials. Despite the loss of jobs, the community supported their own and maintained an air of respectability.

👣

Stop at large granite building facing Monument Square

With the advent of court-mandated school busing in the late 1970s, this genteel setting roiled with uncivil and contentious behavior. One site of confrontation was this austere gray granite building, now a luxurious condominium, which was then **Charlestown High School [15].** The streets exploded in fury when black children were bused to this all-white high school and Charlestown teenagers were sent to schools in black neighborhoods. It took decades to recover racial and moral equilibrium.

Most recently, Charlestown has been experiencing a new wave of immigration—yuppies, who compete with "townies" for living space. The area's strong appeal lies in its small-town congeniality and charming homes, which are more affordable than those of the Back Bay or Beacon Hill. *The Boston Globe* quotes a new resident who cherishes "living in an antique house in a quiet neighborhood where people know each other and look after each other."

The houses bordering the square present a range of 19th-century styles. Consistent rooflines, bay windows punctuating beautifully restored brick façades, and highly polished doors blend harmoniously. One can easily understand why filmmakers Ismail Merchant and James Ivory chose this locale for their movie of Henry James's *The Bostonians.* Conversely, **Cordis Street** is known for its architectural anomalies. Three unusually oriented houses face down the hill, allowing for front yard gardens. These are the oldest on the street, dating from 1790 to 1801. Also on Cordis is an unlikely residence: fronted by four huge Ionic columns, this shabby genteel Greek Revival mansion stands in sharp contrast to its more modest colonial neighbors. The latter constitute what some consider to be Boston's most noteworthy collection of early frame dwellings. The tranquility of the street is unexpected so near a major tourist site.

In contrast is the animated environment of the **Warren Tavern [16],** which has been serving pints for over 200 years and salade niçoise for

Continue to corner of Monument Square and High Street; turn right; make first left; walk down Cordis Street

Turn left on Warren Street, then take the first right onto Pleasant Street.

fewer than 20. Named for the Bunker Hill hero Dr. Joseph Warren, this is the oldest continuously operating tavern in the United States. The original structure dated from 1780; little of that building remained at the time of reconstruction in the 1970s, when it was restored to a worthy facsimile. Its wide floorboards, low ceilings, and worn wooden beams created the cozy environment enjoyed by Paul Revere, George Washington, and other early patriots. Today's patrons are more likely to be locals gathering after work: conversation leans toward the rising cost of living and the unpredictability of the Red Sox rather than taxes on tea and the unpredictability of King George.

👣

Turn right on Main Street to Thompson House

This charming complex of houses at **119 Main Street [17],** with its dazzling central garden, was the homestead of the Thompson family. Timothy Thompson Sr. and his wife were among the first to return to Charlestown after the British retreat. Their son, Timothy Jr., was the first boy to be born in the reestablished community. Diagonally across the street is an 1822 stone building that was owned by local politico General Nathaniel Austin. It is unusual because stone is used very infrequently as construction material in Boston. In fact, the only comparable house is around the corner and was also owned by Austin, who conveniently owned the island from which this unique rubble granite was quarried. Now known as the **Austin Block [18],** it was a store—the local retailer for goods from the West Indies—and for a time the home of Charlestown's first newspaper, *The Bunker Hill Aurora.* The mini-scape of these buildings and the Warren Tavern presents a life-size diorama of Charlestown in the early 19th century.

Savor the colonial ambience punctuated by modern Charlestown. Peek into the dry-cleaning shop that has pragmatically preserved and adapted fixtures from its previous incarnation as Donovan & Fallon Drugs. Hip 21st-century restaurants are juxtaposed with the unadorned **Deacon Larkin House** at **#55 Main Street [19].** Where people emerge from their BMWs today, Paul Revere emerged from the shadows of the Deacon Larkin House more than two centuries ago. This large three-story structure is post-Revolutionary, but historians believe it was built quite near the site where Paul Revere began his famous ride on the eve of the American Revolution. Larkin's claim to fame was that he provided the horse that, unfortunately, was never returned . . . It was commandeered by the British.

Retrace your steps, staying on Main Street; pass the Warren Tavern; stop at 55 Main Street

Elegant **Monument Avenue** perfectly frames the spectacular obelisk of Bunker Hill. Its homes are among the most distinguished of Charlestown. This last photo-op merits a "Wow," especially when the sun is low and bathes the hill in golden light. For an historical "Wow," stop by the **Bunker Hill Museum [20],** housed at the juncture of Monument Avenue and Monument Square. It is replete with dioramas, murals, multimedia exhibits, and a knowledgeable staff.

Retrace steps on Main Street to Monument Avenue; turn right; continue to Monument Square

Retracing your steps to the Navy Yard, it is easier to understand the impossibility of severing Charlestown from Boston—and either of them from the sea. Not only is this an historical impossibility, the sea resides in our DNA. As one of Boston's favorite sons mused . . .

To return to Navy Yard: turn right on Monument Square; bear right onto Winthrop Street; turn left onto Adams Street; continue down hill

I really don't know why it is that all of us are so committed to the sea, except I think it is because in addition to the fact that the sea changes and the light changes, and ships change, it is because we all came from the sea. And it is an interesting biological fact that all of us have, in our veins the exact same percentage of salt in our blood that exists in the ocean, and, therefore, we have salt in our blood, in our sweat, in our tears. We are tied to the ocean. And when we go back to the sea, whether it is to sail or to watch it, we are going back from whence we came.

—*John F. Kennedy, 1962*

It is the sea that sustained Boston, the Navy Yard, and its *pièce de résistance,* the USS *Constitution.* A visit to the ship is highly recommended at this point. U.S. Navy seamen, dressed in 1812 uniforms, lead visitors below deck: on view are the old cannon, and, further below, the cramped quarters where the crew of 200 slept. The guides are informed storytellers, who may or may not elaborate on the following 19th-century sailors' yarn: Although women were forbidden on the ship, an occasional officer's wife was smuggled aboard. Once or twice, very pregnant wives found themselves in a very awkward position. It turns out that the best berth for birthing was the bulkhead, just forward of the guns. And the expression "son of a gun" was born . . .

‼
Return on ferry; note building directly across Boston Harbor

The imposing concave building straight ahead is the **U.S. Courthouse,** built in 1998. Its waterside location is emblematic of its history. The federal court system was founded by George Washington to handle questions of maritime law because these issues often crossed state boundaries, making it difficult to choose the appropriate trial venue.

The building's unique character was forged from different skills and perspectives—federal judges worked with architect Henry N. Cobb to create a structure that not only provided justice but also visually represented it. The goal was to communicate openness through its architectural materials and design. The most obvious and successful statement is the spectacular glass façade, nearly an acre in size. The architect asserted that one of his goals was "to make available to every citizen the extraordinary experience of this splendid site at which, by virtue of its close encounter with downtown Boston, the meeting of city and sea is most vividly dramatized."

It was on the hill marked by the Bunker Hill Monument that the colonists fought for freedom. It was on the USS *Constitution* that the young nation defended itself. And at this new courthouse, Bostonians continue to honor those forefathers who, in the words of Justice Louis D. Brandeis, "valued liberty both as an end and as a means. They believed liberty to be the secret to happiness and courage to be the secret of liberty."

Try to save time to stroll along the harbor's walkway, affording magnificent views of both the city and the sea. The **HarborWalk** extends from Charlestown to the southern end of Boston Harbor. Although at present only 80 percent finished, it already connects six of the city's neighborhoods. Public agencies and private landowners

Addendum:
Debark from ferry;
walk left toward
New England
Aquarium; continue
in same direction
along waterfront

are working together to complete this ambitious 46.9-mile project.

You will follow the coastline into the 21st century. Fish-ophiles should stop at the **New England Aquarium** to see over 2,000 species of fish cavorting, eating, and sleeping in over 200,000 gallons of local saltwater. This dramatic structure, with its four-story fish tank, was one of the first aquariums featuring a multistory natural environment. Designed by the avant-garde Cambridge Seven in 1969, it replaced the 19th-century wharf buildings of Charles Bulfinch (see Beacon Hill Walk), the most revered architect of his time. He also created the now demolished 1805 India Wharf, today the site of I. M. Pei's 1971 luxury condominium **Harbor Towers.** The American Institute of Architects compared the two silhouettes: "In contrast to the historic long low forms of brick, granite and timber extending like fingers into the harbor, Pei's towers introduced a new form and scale to the Boston waterfront." Some observe more pointedly that Pei's buildings relate more to the sky than to the sea. The towers are complemented by the angular planes of David von Schlegell's abstract sculptures, which, appropriately, resemble giant beach chairs.

Continuing past Rowe's Wharf, you approach Fort Point Channel, one of Boston's new "it" destinations. The conversion of this former warehouse area into studios, galleries, lofts, and eateries has attracted the largest population of artists in New England. The new **Institute of Contemporary Art,** sited on the waterfront just beyond the courthouse, anchors this creative community. An "installation in progress" is a new/old **Boston Tea Party Museum.**

If you are tempted to explore further, continue along the HarborWalk. The courthouse welcomes visitors, and its café is open to the public for eat-in or take-away. Should you choose the latter, join the many Bostonians picnicking waterside. The panorama says it all.

MBTA Subway Map

LEGEND

- BLUE LINE
- RED LINE
- GREEN LINE
- ORANGE LINE
- Transit Stops
- Terminal Station
- Free Interchange with other lines

Indoor Foot Notes

The following are our favorite places to meander in inclement weather. Many will keep you occupied—and dry—for at least half a day. Should you get caught in a brief shower, check the indoor recommendations in the Supplements for each walk.

Christian Science Center Mapparium
Step inside this gigantic stained-glass globe to explore the earth's topography.
1 Norway Street, Boston (intersection of Mass. Ave.)

Telephone:	617-450-7000
Hours:	Tues.–Sun., 10:00 A.M.–4:00 P.M.
Admission:	$6; discount seniors and students; under 6, free
Nearest T Stop:	Prudential on Green Line

Gibson House
Typical upper-middle-class Victorian home with period furnishings, textiles, paintings, and fixtures.
137 Beacon Street, Boston, at Berkeley Street

Telephone:	617-267-6338
Hours:	Wed.–Sun., tours at 1:00, 2:00, and 3:00 P.M.
Admission:	$7; discount for seniors, students, and children
Nearest T Stop:	Arlington Street on Green Line

Harvard University Art Museums
Arthur M. Sackler Museum:

Ancient, Asian, and Islamic art, combined with selections from the collections of the Busch Reisinger and Fogg Museums, which are currently under renovation.

485 Broadway, Cambridge, at Quincy Street

Telephone:	617-495-9400
Hours:	Mon.–Sat., 10:00 A.M.– 5:00 P.M.; Sun., 1:00–5:00 P.M.
Admission:	$9; discount for seniors, students, and children; no charge Sat. A.M.
Nearest T Stop:	Harvard Square on Red Line

Harvard Museum of Natural History

One building houses three separate museums—botany, comparative zoology, and mineralogy/geology. The most famous exhibit is the Blaschka glass flowers (more than 830 plant species).

26 Oxford Street, Cambridge, off Kirkland Street

Telephone:	617-495-3045
Hours:	Daily, 9:00 A.M.–5:00 P.M.
Admission:	$9; discount for seniors, students, and children; no charge, Sun. 9:00 A.M.– 12:00 P.M.
Nearest T Stop:	Harvard Square on Red Line

**Peabody Museum of Archaeology
and Ethnology:** Part of the Museum of
Natural History
11 Divinity Avenue, Cambridge, off
Kirkland Street
Hours and admission as above

Institute of Contemporary Art

The most significant national and international
contemporary art is housed in a building that reflects the vigor of the art inside.
100 Northern Avenue, Boston

Telephone:	617-748-3100
Hours:	Tues.–Wed.; Sat.–Sun. 10:00 A.M.–5:00 P.M.; Thurs.–Fri. 10:00 A.M.–9:00 P.M.
Admission:	$12; seniors and students, $10; no charge, Thurs. 5:00–9:00 P.M.
Nearest T Stop:	Courthouse or World Trade Center on Silver Line Water-front (take Red Line to South Station and transfer to Silver Line Waterfront)

Isabella Stewart Gardner Museum

The eccentric art aficionada's Italianate villa houses her eclectic collection, highlighted by paintings by Botticelli, Titian, Rembrandt, Manet, and Rubens. The building itself is a work of art.
280 The Fenway, Boston, between Palace Road and Evans Way

Telephone:	617-566-1401
Hours:	Tues.–Sun., 11:00 A.M.–5:00 P.M.; no admission after 4:20 P.M.
Admission:	$12; discount for seniors and students; under 18, free
Nearest T Stop:	Museum on Green Line (E train); or Huntington Ave. bus #39

John F. Kennedy Library and Museum

Exhibits, tapes, and videos of JFK and his extended family. Frequent special shows; call for current calendar.
Columbia Point off Morrissey Boulevard, next to U Mass–Boston, Dorchester

Telephone:	617-514-1600 or 866-JFK-1960
Hours:	daily, 9:00 A.M.–5:00 P.M.
Admission:	$12; discount for seniors and students; ages 12 and under, free
Nearest T Stop:	JFK/U Mass Boston on Red Line; free shuttle every 20 minutes

Museum of African American History

Exhibits and videos about African American history in New England

8 Smith Court, Boston, off Joy Street, between Cambridge and Myrtle Streets

Telephone:	617-725-0022
Hours:	Mon.–Sat., 10:00 A.M.–4:00 P.M.
Admission:	free; suggested donation, $5
Nearest T Stop:	Charles Street/MGH on Red Line

Museum of Fine Arts

It's all here—one of America's great museums, with an especially strong collection of American art and furniture.

465 Huntington Avenue, Boston, between Forsyth Way and Museum Road

Telephone:	617-267-9300
Hours:	Sat.–Tues., 10:00 A.M.–4:45 P.M.; Wed.–Fri., 10:00 A.M.–9:45 P.M.
Admission:	$17; discount for seniors and students over 18; ages 17 and under, $6.50, and free weekdays after 3:00 P.M., weekends, and school holidays; Wed. after 4:00 P.M., by donation
Nearest T Stop:	Museum on Green Line

Museums at MIT

MIT Museum: Science and technology, both historic and futuristic

265 Mass. Ave., Cambridge, at Front Street

Telephone:	617-253-5927
Hours:	daily, 10:00 A.M.–5:00 P.M.
Admission:	$7.50 adults; $3 children
Nearest T Stop:	Kendall/MIT on Red Line

Hart Nautical Gallery: Model ships and plans

Rogers Building, 55 Mass. Ave., Cambridge, near Memorial Drive

Telephone:	617-253-5942
Hours:	daily, 9:00 A.M.–5:00 P.M.
Admission:	free
Nearest T Stop:	Kendall/MIT on Red Line

Museum of Science

From *Tyrannosaurus rex* to space travel; includes Hayden Planetarium and Mugar Omni Theater (check for show times and admissions)

Monsignor O'Brien Highway, Cambridge, between Charles Street and Commercial Avenue

Telephone:	617-723-2500
Hours:	July 5–Labor Day: Sat.–Thurs., 9:00 A.M.–7:00 P.M.; Fri., 9:00 A.M.–9:00 P.M.; Rest of year: Sat.–Thurs., 9:00 A.M.–5:00; Fri., 9:00 A.M.–9:00 P.M.
Admission:	$19; discount for seniors, students, and children
Nearest T Stop:	Science Park on Green Line

Trinity Church

One of the top ten architectural sites in America

Copley Square, Boston

Telephone:	617-536-0944
Hours:	Tues.–Sat., 9:00 A.M.–6:00 P.M.; docent-led tours, call for schedule
Admission:	$6; discount for seniors and students
Nearest T Stop:	Copley Square on Green Line

Selected Bibliography

Amory, Cleveland. *The Proper Bostonians.* New York: E. P. Dutton, 1947.

Harris, John. *Historic Walks in Old Boston,* 4th ed. Guilford, CT: Globe Pequot Press, 2000.

Hogarth, Paul. *Walking Tours of Old Boston.* New York: E. P. Dutton, 1978.

Kay, Jane Holtz. *Lost Boston.* New York: Houghton Mifflin, 1999.

Lyndon, Donlyn. *The City Observed: Boston.* New York: Vintage Books, 1982.

Morison, Samuel Eliot. *One Boy's Boston.* Cambridge, MA: Riverside Press, 1962.

O'Connor, Thomas H. *Boston A to Z.* Cambridge, MA: Harvard University Press, 2000.

Shand-Tucci, Douglass. *Harvard University.* New York: Princeton Architectural Press, 2001.

Schlesinger, Marian Cannon. *Snatched from Oblivion.* Boston: Little, Brown, 1979.

Weston, George F. Jr. *Boston Ways.* Boston: Beacon Press, 1957.

Whitehill, Walter Muir, and Lawrence W. Kennedy. *Boston: A Topographical History.* Cambridge, MA: Belknap Press, 2000.

Wilson, Susan. *Literary Trail of Greater Boston.* Boston: Houghton Mifflin, 2000.

Yee, Chiang. *The Silent Traveller in Boston.* New York: W. W. Norton, 1959.

Index

About the authors

Jane Grossman and Felice Yager were introduced ten years ago by a mutual friend who knew they were both avid walkers. Their friendship developed during long morning walks along the Charles River, in snow and sun. They soon discovered their common interest in travel, writing, and social history.

Ms. Grossman is a cofounder of the former Traveller's Bookstore in New York City, which sold guidebooks, fiction, and nonfiction; published a travel-book catalog; and published guidebooks. When she moved to the Boston area in late 1997, she looked in vain for a good walking guide to her new hometown. She found Ms. Yager instead.

Ms. Yager, a psychologist, worked for many years with immigrants to Boston, helping them adjust and become oriented in their new city. Much of her career has been devoted to social service, and consequently she is an experienced writer of fiction—specializing in grants.